The Hand-knitted Nursery

The Hand-knitted Nursery

35 GORGEOUS DESIGNS FOR FURNISHINGS, CLOTHES, AND TOYS

Melanie Porter

CICO BOOKS

LONDON NEW YORK

I'd like to dedicate this book to my own son, Jai, who has filled our world with joy and plastic toys. And who patiently waited to be born until a few days after the hand-in of the book projects.

Published in 2014 by CICO Books
An imprint of Ryland Peters & Small
519 Broadway, 5th Floor,
New York NY 10012
20–21 Jockey's Fields,
London WC1R 4BW
www.rylandpeters.com

10 9 8 7 6 5 4 3 2 1

A CIP catalog record for this book is available from the Library of Congress and the British Library.

ISBN: 978-1-78249-090-6

Printed in China

Editor: Kate Haxell
Designer: Elizabeth Healey
Pattern checker: Susan Horan
Illustrators: Kuo Kang Chen, Stephen Dew, and Kate Simunek
Photographers: Emma Mitchell and Matthew Dickens (page 108)
Stylist: Nel Haynes and Sophie Martell

Contents

Introduction

My hand-knitted homewares brand stems from an interest in using knitted materials to create contemporary home furnishings. Using traditional and unusual materials, such as merino wool and sailor's rope, I like to experiment with contrasts in scale and texture. My first book, *Hand-Knit Your Home*, translates many of the products from my collection into hand knits for you to make for your own interiors.

Knitting often invokes a sense of nostalgia and it is this seeking of comfort in the past that has inspired my second book. Growing up in a family of craftsmen I was always surrounded by handmade toys, and sewing and knitting projects were always keeping hands busy. Many of the projects in this book have their origins in items that I remember from my childhood—from a papier mâché hot-air balloon hanging from my ceiling that has been redesigned into a knitted project (see page 100), to a vintage, sewn coat hanger cover that inspired my charming cat coat hanger (see page 72).

I have designed 35 projects that I hope will excite and inspire you to knit for both a baby's nursery and a toddler's bedroom. These include clothes that could be a perfect gift for a newborn, and larger projects that will become family heirlooms.

CHAPTER ONE

Baby's Room

Soft pastels and snuggly yarns make lovely things for your nursery, and for your baby. Knit pieces to keep a tiny person cozy, including mittens and a papoose, and make simple but sweet room decorations.

Cable hat

This pretty little cable hat coordinates perfectly with the mittens and bootees (see pages 12 and 40). The contrast trim frames a baby's captivating face, while the graduated cable makes this a nicely challenging project.

Skill level ★★★

Size

0–6 months: 17in (43cm) circumference x 4¾in (12cm) height

→ **KNITTING IN THE ROUND**

This technique can feel awkward at the start, but persevere as it will get easier as you increase the number of stitches on your needles.

Materials

Yarn

Double knit yarn such as Baby Merino Silk DK from Rowan—66% merino, 34% tussah silk; approx. 147yds (135m) per 1¾oz (50g) ball

- Teal (A)—¾oz (20g)/58yds (54m)
- Bluebird (B)—¼oz (10g)/29yds (27m)

OR

- Shell Pink (A)—¾oz (20g)/58yds (54m)
- Rose (B)—¼oz (10g)/29yds (27m)

Needles

Set of five US 6 (4mm) double-pointed knitting needles

Other materials

- Cable needle
- Knitter's sewing needle

Gauge (tension)

23 sts and 29 rows to 4in (10cm) over cable patt using US 6 (4mm) needles

Abbreviations

C4Finc2—cable 4 front increase 2 sts: slip next 2 sts onto cable needle and hold at front of work, knit next 2 sts from left-hand needle, make 2 sts, then knit 2 sts from cable needle

C6F—cable 6 forward: slip next 3 sts onto cable needle and hold at front of work, knit next 3 sts from left-hand needle, then knit 3 sts from cable needle

See also page 126

Pattern

Hat

Using A, cast on 8 sts.

Evenly distribute sts over 4 double-pointed needles and ensuring work is not twisted, cont in rounds. Place a stitch marker to denote end of round.

Round 1: [K1, m1] to end. *16 sts*

Round 2: [K1, m1] to end. *32 sts*

Round 3: Knit.

Round 4: [K4, m1p] to end. *40 sts*

Round 5: [K4, p1] to end.

Round 6: [C4Finc2, m1p, p1] to end.
64 sts

Round 7: [K6, p2] to end.

Round 8: [K6, p1, m1p, p1] to end.
72 sts

Round 9: [K6, p3] to end.

Round 10: [K6, p1, m1p, p2] to end.
80 sts

Rounds 11 – 12: [K6, p4] to end.

Round 13: [K6, p2, m1p, p2] to end.
88 sts

Round 14: [K6, p5] to end.

Round 15: [C6F, p5] to end.

Rounds 16 – 23: [K6, p5] to end.

Round 24: [C6F, p5] to end.

Rounds 25 – 31: [K6, p5] to end.
Change to B.

Round 32: Knit.

Round 33: Purl.

Rep rounds 32–33 once more, then rep
round 32 once more.
Bind (cast) off.

To make up

• Gather cast-on stitches securely.

• Weave in loose ends.

• Steam lightly.

Mini mittens

Quick and simple to make, these dainty mittens are perfect as a newborn gift. They have crochet-chain ties to keep them on tiny hands. Why not try making a set of three in different colors?

12

Skill level ★★

Size
Newborn: 3½ x 2½in (9 x 6cm)

Materials

Yarn
Double knit yarn such as Baby Merino Silk DK from Rowan—66% merino, 34% tussah silk; approx. 147yds (135m) per 1¾ oz (50g) ball

- Teal (A)— ¼ oz (10g)/29yds (27m)
- Bluebird (B)— ½ oz (14g)/44yds (40m)

OR

- Shell Pink (A)— ¼ oz (10g)/29yds (27m)
- Rose (B)— ½ oz (14g)/44yds (40m)

Needles
Pair of US 6 (4mm) knitting needles

Other materials
- Knitter's sewing needle
- Cable needle
- G/6 (4mm) crochet hook

Gauge (tension)
23 sts and 29 rows to 4in (10cm) over cable patt using US 6 (4mm) needles

→ SHORT-ROW SHAPING

To stop a hole forming at the turn in a short row, with the yarn in front, slip the next stitch after the turn onto the right-hand needle. Wrap the yarn around the slipped stitch to the back. Slip the stitch back onto the left-hand needle. Turn and continue knitting in the opposite direction.

Row 4: P3, k2, p4, k2, p4, k6.

Row 5: K10, p2, k4, p2, k2, turn.

Row 6: P2, k2, p4, k2, p4, k6.

Row 7: K10, p2, k4, p2, k1, turn.

Row 8: P1, k2, p4, k2, p4, k6.

Row 9: K4, yo, k2tog, k4, p2, C4F, p2, turn.

Row 10: K2, p4, k2, p4, k6.

Row 11: As row 7.

Row 12: As row 8.

Row 13: As row 5.

Row 14: As row 6.

Row 15: As row 3.

Row 16: As row 4.

Row 17: K4, yo, k2tog, k4, p2, C4F, p2, k4.

Row 18: As row 2.

Rep rows 1 – 18.

Bind (cast) off.

Cord (make 2)

Using B, make a crochet chain approx. 12in (30cm) long.

To make up

• Weave in all loose ends.
• Join seam in mitten using knitting yarn.
• Thread cord through eyelets.

Abbreviations

C4F—cable 4 front: slip next 2 sts onto cable needle and hold at front of work, knit next 2 sts from left-hand needle, then knit 2 sts from cable needle

See also page 126

Pattern

Mitten (make 2)

Using A, cast on 22 sts.

Row 1: K10, p2, k4, p2, k4.

Row 2: P4, k2, p4, k2, p4, k6.

Row 3: K10, p2, k4, p2, k3, turn.

Planet mobile

Keep your baby entertained with a mobile which is out of this world! You could make this project in colors from your nursery to create a bespoke piece.

Skill level ★★

Size

Variable, depending on spacing between the planets

Materials

Yarn

Scraps of double knit yarn (any type will work) in colors to suit

- Circular ring—approx. ¼ oz (10g)
- Small planet—approx. ¼ oz (10g)
- Large planet—approx. ¼ oz (10g)

Needles

Pair each of US 5 (3.75mm) and US 3 (3.25mm) knitting needles

Other materials

- One 6¾ in (17cm) polystyrene ring
- Four 2in (5cm) polystyrene balls
- One 4in (10cm) polystyrene ball
- Knitter's sewing needle
- Fishing line
- Curtain ring for hanging

Gauge (tension)

22 sts and 32 rows to 4in (10cm) over st st using US 3 (3.25mm) needles

21 sts and 29 rows to 4in (10cm) over st st using US 5 (3.75mm) needles

Abbreviations

See page 126

Pattern

Circular ring

Using US 5 (3.75mm) needles, cast on 16 sts.

Row 1: Knit.

Row 2: Purl.

Rows 3–20: Work in st st.

Row 21: K12, turn.

Row 22: P8, turn.

Row 23: K12.

Row 24: Purl.

Rep rows 3–24, 6 more times.

Bind (cast) off, taking needle through corresponding st on cast-on edge as you work, to form a circle. Fasten off, leaving long end for sewing seam.

Small planet (make 4)

Using US 3 (3.25mm) needles, cast on 7 sts.

Row 1: K1, [inc] in every st to end. *13 sts*

Row 2 and every alt row: Purl.

Row 3: [Inc] in every st to end. *26 sts*

Row 5: [Inc, k1] to end. *39 sts*

Rows 6–16: Work in st st.

Row 17: [K2tog, k1] to end. *26 sts*

Row 19: [K2tog] to end. *13 sts*

Row 21: K1, [k2tog] to end. *7 sts*

Cut yarn, leaving a long end, and thread through rem sts, drawing tight to close. Do not fasten off.

Large planet

Using US 3 (3.25mm) needles, cast on 12 sts.

Row 1: Knit.

Row 2 and every alt row: Purl.

Row 3: [Inc] in every st to end. *24 sts*

Row 5: [Inc, k1] to end. *36 sts*

Row 7: K1, [inc, k2] 11 times, inc, k1. *48 sts*

Row 9: [Inc, k3] to end. *60 sts*

Row 11: [Inc, k4] to end. *72 sts*

Rows 12–36: Work in st st.

Row 37: [K4, k2tog] to end. *60 sts*

Row 39: [K3, k2tog] to end. *48 sts*

Row 41: K1, k2tog, [k2, k2tog] to last st, k1. *36 sts*

Row 43: [K1, k2tog] to end. *24 sts*

Row 45: [K2tog] to end. *12 sts*

Row 47: [K2tog] to end. *6 sts*

Cut yarn, leaving a long end, and thread through rem sts, drawing tight to close. Do not fasten off.

To make up

- Wrap circular ring piece of knitting round polystyrene ring and sew seam closed on inside using long end.
- Wrap small planet pieces of knitting around 2in (5cm) balls and stitch seam closed using long end.
- Wrap large planet piece of knitting around 4in (10cm) polystyrene ball and stitch seam closed using knitting yarn.
- Using lengths of fishing line, hang balls from circular ring at required drops.
- Use three evenly spaced lengths of fishing line to hang circular ring from curtain ring, which can be used to hang mobile from ceiling hook.

NB: Ensure that you increase the height of the mobile above the crib before your baby is able to sit up or pull themselves up using the bars of the crib.

→ ADDING COLOR

Insert a contrast color by changing yarns, though just follow the instructions for single color pattern for the shaping.

15

Corsage wall decoration

Hang this decoration on the door or wall of a little girl's room, or even your own bedframe, to give a feminine touch. It also provides a great way to use up scraps of yarn in your stash.

Skill level ★★

Size

12in (30cm) diameter

Materials

Yarn

Chunky yarn such as Cocoon from Rowan—80% merino, 20% kid mohair: approx. 126yds (115m) per 3½ oz (100g) ball

• Kiwi—approx. 3½ oz (100g)/ 126yds (115m)

Scraps of DK and chunky yarns for flowers

• Approx. ¾ oz (20g)/ 25yds (23m) per flower

Needles

Set of four double-pointed US 8 (5mm) knitting needles

Other materials

• 10in (25cm) polystyrene half ring
• Knitter's sewing needle
• E/4 (3.5mm) and H/8 (4.5mm) crochet hooks
• Mattress needle

Gauge (tension)

13 sts and 19 rows to 4in (10cm) over st st using US 8 (5mm) needles

Abbreviations

See page 126

Pattern

Ring

Cast on 70 sts.

Evenly distribute sts over 3 double-pointed needles. Place a marker to denote end of round.

Rounds 1–6: Knit.

Round 7: [K4, inc] to end. *84 sts*

Rounds 8–9: Knit.

Round 10: [K5, inc] to end. *98 sts*

Rounds 11–12: Knit.

Round 13: [K6, inc] to end. *112 sts*

Rounds 14–20: Knit.

Round 21: [K6, k2tog] to end. *98 sts*

Rounds 22–23 Knit.

Round 24: [K5, k2tog] to end. *84 sts*

Rounds 25–26: Knit.

Round 27: [K4, k2tog] to end. *70 sts*

US crochet terms are used in this pattern; the UK equivalents are on page 122. The flowers are all made from the same pattern; different thicknesses of yarn create different-sized flowers. I used an E/4 (3.5mm) crochet hook for DK yarn and a H/8 (4.5mm) for chunky yarn.

→ FLOWERS

Round 28: Knit.
Bind (cast) off.

Flower (make as many as wanted)

Ch27.

Row 1: 2dc (tr) in 2nd ch from hook ch, 2dc (tr) in each ch to end. *52dc (tr)*

Row 2: [Ch3, 1sc (dc) in 4th dc (tr) 13 times.

Row 3: [1sc (dc), 3dc (tr), 1 sc (dc)] in each of first 3 ch spaces, [1 sc (dc), 1dc (tr), 3tr (dtr), 1dc (tr), 1 sc (dc)] in rem ch spaces. *13 petals*

Fasten off.

To make up

- Stretch knitting over polystyrene ring and join seam on inside rim.
- Curl each flower strip into a flower shape, with the smallest petals in the center, and use matching yarn to sew the layers together on the back of the flower, leaving a long end.
- Attach the flowers in position on the ring using the mattress needle through the polystyrene ring and secure on the back.

Baby blanket

With a pretty scalloped edge and beautiful pattern on both sides, this newborn blanket is set to become a family heirloom. Once you get the hang of the pattern, the repeat makes this a great project to work on in the evening or when on the move.

Skill level ★★★

Size
25¼ x 21¼in (64 x 54cm)

Materials
Yarn
Double knit yarn such as Baby Merino Silk DK from Rowan—66% merino, 34% tussah silk; approx. 147yds (135m) per 1¾oz (50g) ball
• Rose—approx. 7oz (200g)/600yds (540m)

Needles
Pair of US 7 (4.5mm) knitting needles

Other materials
• Knitter's sewing needle

Gauge (tension)
25 sts and 30 rows to 4in (10cm) over patt using US 7 (4.5mm) needles

Abbreviations
See page 126

Pattern
Main piece
Cast on 161 sts.
Row 1 (RS): P1, [k1, p1, k5, p1] to end.
Row 2: K1, [p5, k1, p1, k1] to end.
Row 3: P1, [m1, (k1, p1, k1) all in next st, m1, p1, k5tog, p1] to end.
Row 4: K1, [p1, k1, p5, k1] to end.
Row 5: P1, [k5, p1, k1, p1] to end.
Rep rows 4–5 once more, then rep row 4 once more.
Row 9: P1, [k5tog, p1, m1, (k1, p1, k1) all in next st, m1, p1] to end.
Rep row 2 once more, then rep rows 1–2 once more.
Rep these 12 rows, 12 more times, then rep rows 1–5 once more.
Bind (cast) off in patt.

To make up
• Weave in loose ends.
• Steam lightly.

Row 79: Work 10 sts seed (moss) st, p29, [k1, p1] 6 times, p29, work 10 sts seed (moss) st.

Rep rows 76–78 once more.

Row 83: Work 10 sts seed (moss) st, p29, [k1, p1] 3 times; put rem 45 sts onto a stitch holder and cont on these 45 sts only.

Row 84: Work 6 sts seed (moss) st, [k1, p1, k1] all into next st, [p3tog, (k1, p1, k1) all into next st] to last 10 sts, work 10 sts seed (moss) st.

Row 85: Work 10 sts seed (moss) st, p to last 6 sts, work 6 sts seed (moss) st.

Row 86: Work 6 sts seed (moss) st, p3tog, [[k1, p1, k1] all into next st, p3tog] to last 10 sts, work 10 sts seed (moss) st.

Row 87: As row 85.

Rep rows 84–87, 21 more times.

Work 14 rows seed (moss) st.

Bind (cast) off.

With RS facing, slip sts from holder on to needle.

Row 83: Work 6 sts seed (moss) st, p to last 10 sts, work 10 sts seed (moss) st.

Row 84: Work 10 sts seed (moss) st, [k1, p1, k1] all into next st, [p3tog, (k1, p1, k1) all into next st] to last 6 sts, work 6 sts seed (moss) st.

Row 85: Work 6 sts seed (moss) st, p to last 10 sts, work 10 sts seed (moss) st.

Row 86: Work 10 sts seed (moss) st, p3tog, [[k1, p1, k1] all into next st, p3tog] to last 6 sts, work 6 sts seed (moss) st.

Row 87: As row 85.

Rep rows 84–87, 21 more times.

Work 14 rows seed (moss) st.

Bind (cast) off.

To make up

- Weave in all loose ends.
- Steam flat and shape into rectangle.

Row 76: Work 10 sts seed (moss) st, [k1, p1, k1] all into next st, [p3tog, (k1, p1, k1) all into next st] 7 times, [p1, k1] 6 times, (k1, p1, k1) all into next st, [p3tog, (k1, p1, k1) all into next st] 7 times, work 10 sts seed (moss) st.

Row 77: Work 10 sts seed (moss) st, p31, [k1, p1] 6 times, p31, work 10 sts seed (moss) st.

Row 78: Work 10 sts seed (moss) st, p3tog, [[k1, p1, k1] all into next st, p3tog] 7 times, [k1, p1] 6 times, p3tog, [[k1, p1, k1] all into next st, p3tog] 7 times, work 10 sts seed (moss) st.

Snuggle bunny

A lovely simple shape and knitted in a super-soft yarn, this cute bunny toy makes an ideal gift! This project is knitted with both a single end of yarn and double ends to give different textures.

Skill level ★★

Size
6 x 4in (15 x 10cm)

Materials

Yarn

Soft DK yarn, such as Baby Alpaca from King Cole—100% baby alpaca: approx. 110yds (100m) per 1¾oz (50g) ball
- Camel—1oz (30g)/65yds (60m)
- Small amount of white for tail

Needles
Pair each of US 2 (2.75mm) and US 6 (4mm) knitting needles

Other materials
- Knitter's sewing needle
- Stitch holder
- Toy stuffing
- Scraps of brown and pink yarn for features

Gauge (tension)
26 sts and 33 rows to 4in (10cm) over st st using US 2 (2.75mm) needles

Abbreviations
See page 126

Pattern

Front

Using US 2 (2.75mm) needles, cast on 34 sts.

Row 1 (RS): K2, [p2, k2] to end.

Rows 2–3: Inc, work every st in patt as it presents to last st, inc. *38 sts*

Rows 4–5: Work every st in patt as it presents.

Row 6: K2togtbl, work every st in patt as it presents to last 2 sts, k2tog. *36 sts*

Rows 7–9: Work every st in patt as it presents.

Row 10: P2tog, work every st in patt as it presents to last 2 sts, p2togtbl. *34 sts*

Rows 11–13: Work every st in patt as it presents.

Row 14: P2tog, work every st in patt as it presents to last 2 sts, p2togtbl. *32 sts*

Rows 15–16: Work every st in patt as it presents.

Row 17: P2tog, work every st in patt as it presents to last 2 sts, p2togtbl. *30 sts*

Rows 18–25: Work every st in patt as it presents.

Row 26: Inc, work every st in patt as it presents to last st, inc. *32 sts*

Rows 27–33: Work every st in patt as it presents.

Row 34: Work 14 sts in patt as they present, k2tog, slip rem 16 sts onto stitch holder.

→ FOR SMALL BABIES

Washing the finished knitting will remove some of the loose fibers, but in case any fibers are still shed, it is best not to give the bunny to babies under a year old.

First ear

Cont on 15 sts on needles.

Rows 35–39: Work every st in patt as it presents.

Row 40: Work 13 sts in patt as they present, k2tog. *14 sts*

Rows 41–43: Work every st in patt as it presents.

Row 44: Work 12 sts in patt as they present, p2togtbl. *13 sts*

Rows 45–46: Work every st in patt as it presents.

Row 47: K2togtbl, work 9 sts in patt as they present, p2togtbl. *11 sts*

Row 48: Work every st in patt as it presents.

Row 49: K1, [p2tog, k2tog] twice, p2tog. *6 sts*

Bind (cast) off in rib.

Second ear

With RS facing, slip stitches from holder onto US 6 (4mm) needle so point of needle is in center of knitting. Rejoin yarn.

Row 1 (WS): K2togtbl, work rem sts in patt as they present. *15 sts*

Rows 2–6: Work every st in patt as it presents.

Row 7: K2togtbl, work 13 sts in patt as they present. *14 sts*

Rows 8–10: Work every st in patt as it presents.

Row 11: P2tog, work 12 sts in patt as they present. *13 sts*

Rows 12–13: Work every st in patt as it presents.

Row 14: P2tog, work 9 sts in patt as they present, k2tog. *11 sts*

Row 15: Work every st in patt as it presents.

Row 16: [P2tog, k2tog] twice, p2tog, k1. *6 sts*

Bind (cast) off in rib.

Back

Using TWO ENDS of yarn held together and US 6 (4mm) needles, cast on 18 sts.

Row 1 (RS): Knit.

Row 2: Inc, p to last st, inc. *20 sts*

Rows 3–4: Work in st st.

Row 5: K2togtbl, k16, k2tog. *18 sts*

Rows 6–8: Work in st st.

Row 9: K2togtbl, k14, k2tog. *16 sts*

Rows 10–12: Work in st st.

Row 13: K2togtbl, k12, k2tog. *14 sts*

Rows 14–19: Work in st st.

Row 20: Inc, p to last st, inc. *16 sts*

Rows 21–24: Work in st st.

Row 25: K6, k2tog, slip rem 8 sts onto stitch holder.

First ear

Cont on 7 sts on needles.

Rows 26–29: Work in st st.

Row 30: P2tog, p5. *6 sts*

Rows 31–34: Work in st st.

Row 35: K2togtbl, k2, k2tog. *4 sts*

Bind (cast) off.

Second ear

With RS facing, slip stitches from holder onto US 6 (4mm) needle so point of needle is in center of knitting. Rejoin yarn.

Row 1 (RS): K2togtbl, k6. *7 sts*

Rows 2–5: Work in st st.

Row 6: P5, p2togtbl. *6 sts*

Rows 7–10: Work in st st.

Row 11: K2togtbl, k2, k2tog. *4 sts*

Bind (cast) off.

Base

Using TWO ENDS of yarn held together and US 6 (4mm) needles, cast on 18 sts.

Row 1 (RS): Knit.

Row 2: Inc, p18, inc. *20 sts*

Rows 3–9: Work in st st.

Row 10: P2tog, p16, p2togtbl. *18 sts*

Row 11: Knit.

Bind (cast) off.

Tail

Using white yarn and US 2 (2.75mm) needles, cast on 8 sts.

Row 1 (RS) and every alt row: Purl.

Row 2: Inc, k6, inc. *10 sts*

Row 4: Inc, k8, inc. *12 sts*

Row 6: Inc, k10, inc. *14 sts*

Row 8: Knit.

Row 10: K2togtbl, k10, k2tog. *12 sts*

Row 12: K2togtbl, k8, k2tog. *10 sts*

Row 14: K2togtbl, k6, k2tog. *8 sts*

Bind (cast) off leaving a long end.

To make up

- Weave in all loose ends.
- Wash the knitting gently and leave to dry.
- Using the long end, sew round the bunny tail just inside the edge of the circle and pull up to make ball. Secure end of yarn.

- Using knitting yarn sew front to back, leaving the bottom open below the first increase.
- Sew base to front edge.
- Sew tail to back securely.
- Stuff bunny with soft toy stuffing, then sew up opening.
- Using scraps of yarn, embroider face as in photograph.

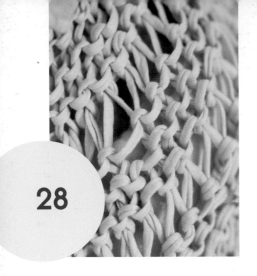

Storage pouch

This knitted storage pouch is ideal for keeping cloths or cotton wool tidied away, yet still easily to hand. The jersey yarn comes in many different colors, so you could make two or three pouches to use around the house.

Skill level ★

Size

Height 14in (35cm); circumference 25in (64cm)

Materials

Yarn

Stretchy jersey fabric yarn such as Hooplayarn from Hoopla—100% cotton jersey; approx. 110yds (100m) per 17½oz (500g) ball

• Pale Peach—approx. 8¾oz (250g)/55yds (50m)

Needles

Pair of US 15 (10mm) knitting needles

Other materials

• Large crochet hook

• Bodkin

Gauge (tension)

9 sts and 12 rows to 3½in (9cm) over patt using US 15 (10mm) needles

Abbreviations

See page 126

Pattern

Main piece

Cast on 9 sts.

Row 1: K1, [yo, k1] to end. *17 sts*

Row 2: [Yo2] to end.

Row 3: Knit, dropping extra loop on each st.

Rows 4–6: Knit.

Row 7: K1, [yo, k1] to end. *33 sts*

Rep rows 2–6 once.

Row 13: K1, [yo, k1] to end. *65 sts*

Rep rows 2–6 once.

Row 19: Knit.

Rows 20–24: Rep rows 2–6 once.

Rep rows 19–24 twice.

Row 37: K21, [k2tog, k5] 3 times, k2tog, k21. *61 sts*

Rep rows 2–3 once.

Rows 40–41: Knit.

Row 42: K19, [k2tog, k5] 3 times, k2tog, k19. *57 sts*

Rows 43–45: Knit.

Row 46: K17, [k2tog, k5] 3 times, k2tog, k17. *53 sts*

Row 47: Knit.

Bind (cast) off.

To make up

• Use the knitting yarn to draw together the cast-on edge and join the side seam to make a bowl shape. Make a crochet chain approximately 4in (10cm) in length and attach to top of seam as hanging loop.

→ **THE YARN**

Because this yarn is made from off-cuts from the textile industry, the stretch can vary depending on the fabric that was used to make it. This will affect the gauge (tension), but don't worry too much about it—just knit to your natural gauge (tension).

Covered basket

I love using unusual yarns and contrasts in textures. A wicker basket and jersey yarn combine perfectly to create a stylish project, ideal for keeping toys and other nursery bits and pieces tidied away!

30

Skill level ★

Size
5½ x 14in (14 x 36cm)

Materials

Yarn
A stretchy jersey fabric yarn such as Hooplayarn from Hoopla—100% cotton jersey; approx. 110yds (100m) per 17½oz (500g) ball
• Pale Peach—approx. 8¾oz (250g)/55yds (50m)

Needles
Pair of US 10½ (6.5mm) knitting needles

Other materials
• Basket measuring 5½in (14cm) tall by 14in (36cm) in diameter
• Satinwood paint (optional)
• Paintbrush (optional)
• Bodkin
• Strong matching sewing thread
• Sewing needle

Gauge (tension)
10 sts and 14 rows to 4in (10cm) over patt using US 10½ (6.5mm) needles

Abbreviations
See page 126

→ PAINTING THE BASKET

If you want to change the color of your basket, you can paint the wicker with satinwood paint: I chose to paint my basket white.

Pattern

Main piece

Cast on 15 sts.

Row 1: K1, p1, k1, turn.

Row 2: K1, p1, k1.

Row 3: [K1, p1] 3 times, turn.

Row 4: [P1, k1] to end.

Row 5: [K1, p1] 4 times, k1, turn.

Row 6: [K1, p1] to last st, k1.

Row 7: [K1, p1] 6 times, turn.

Row 8: [P1, k1] to end.

Rows 9 – 12: [K1, p1] 7 times, k1.

Rep rows 1 – 12, 19 more times.

To make up

• Using the knitting yarn, graft the cast-on row to the final row to create a tube.

• Weave in all loose ends.

• Stitch one edge of the knitted tube to the top of the basket by passing the needle and thread through the edge of the knitting and under the top edge of the basket.

• Run a length of knitting yarn around the free edge of the tube to create a drawstring closure.

Knit fabric pom-poms

I just couldn't resist putting these gorgeous pom-poms made out of jersey knit fabric in this book, even though they aren't actually knitted! Hang them in a cluster, as here, or you could use them individually.

Skill level ★

Size
Approx. 6¼ in (16cm) in diameter

Materials
Yarn
• Jersey knit fabric cut into long strips approx. ½ in (1.5cm) wide

Other materials
• Two card pom-pom templates (see page 126)
• Sharp fabric scissors

Pattern
Take one long strip of jersey fabric and lay it around the inside circle of one template. Place the second template on top to make a sandwich, matching the gaps in the cardboard so that the is a space to pass the fabric through. The strip of fabric between the boards will be used to pull the pom-pom tight and secure it.

Take each strip in turn and wrap it around the template sandwich, overlapping the previous wrap each time, and pulling the fabric so that it stretches slightly.

Wrap all the way around the template until there are four layers of fabric covering every part of the cardboard.

Pull the sandwich strip (the one between the two templates) tighter and keep the ends long so you can identify them later.

Holding all the layers in place with one hand, insert the tip of sharp scissors between the two templates and cut carefully all the way around.

Once all the ends are cut, draw the sandwich strip as tight as possible and secure with a firm double knot.

Trim any longer ends so that you have a neat round ball, and fluff it up.

Hang the pom-pom from the long end.

→ GROUPS OF POM-POMS

Make two or three pom-poms in different fabrics, or using different-sized templates, to create a cluster.

BABY'S ROOM → KNIT FABRIC POM-POMS

Chair cushions

This pattern can be easily adapted to update a tired piece of furniture with Aran knit cushions. I used a modern rocking chair, which contrasts particularly well with the traditional style of the knitting.

Skill level ★★

Size

Seat cushion: approx. 25½in (65cm) wide x 29½in (75cm) deep.
Back cushion: approx. 25½in (65cm) wide x 20in (51cm) deep

Materials

Yarn

A chunky wool yarn, such as Wool City Wool Super Chunky from Texere—100% wool; approx. 220yds (200m) per 14oz (400g) cone

- Ecru—3.5lbs (1.6kgs)/880yds (800m)

Needles

Pair of US 10½ (6.5mm) knitting needles

Other materials

- Chair with removable cushions: seat cushion measuring 25½in (65cm) wide x 29½in (75cm) deep and back cushion measuring 25½in (65cm) wide x 20in (51cm) deep
- Canvas or similar fabric for base of seat cushion
- Cable needle
- Knitter's sewing needle
- Strong matching sewing thread
- Sewing needle

Gauge (tension)

11 sts and 14 rows to 4in (10cm) over st st using US 10½ (6.5mm) needles

Abbreviations

C4B—cable 4 back: slip next 2 sts onto cable needle and hold at back of work, knit next 2 sts from left-hand needle, then knit 2 sts from cable needle

C4F—cable 4 front: slip next 2 sts onto cable needle and hold at front of work, knit next 2 sts from left-hand needle, then knit 2 sts from cable needle

C3L—cable 3 left: slip next 2 sts onto cable needle and hold at front of work, purl next st from left-hand needle, then knit 2 sts from cable needle

C3R—cable 3 right: slip next st onto cable needle and hold at back of work, knit next 2 sts from left-hand needle, then purl st from cable needle

See also page 126

Pattern

Seat pad

Cast on 68 sts.

Row 1: [P2, k2] 4 times, p6, [k2, p8, k2] twice, p6, [k2, p2] 4 times.

Row 2 and every alt row: Work every st in patt as it presents.

Row 3: [P2, k2] 4 times, p6, k2, p8, C4F, p8, k2, p6, [k2, p2] 4 times.

Row 25: [P2, k2] 4 times, p6, [C3R, p6, C3L] twice, p6, [k2, p2] 4 times.

Row 27: [P2, k2] 4 times, p6, k2, p8, C4F, p8, k2, p6, [k2, p2] 4 times.

Row 28: Work every st in patt as it presents.

Rep rows 1–28, 3 more times.

Bind (cast) off.

Seat back (make 2)

Cast on 60 sts.

Row 1: [P2, k2] 3 times, p6, [k2, p8, k2] twice, p6, [k2, p2] 3 times.

Row 2 and every alt row: Work every st in patt as it presents.

Row 3: [P2, k2] 3 times, p6, k2, p8, C4F, p8, k2, p6, [k2, p2] 3 times.

Row 5: [P2, k2] 3 times, p6, [C3L, p6, C3R] twice, p6, [k2, p2] 3 times.

Row 7: [P2, k2] 3 times, p6, [p1, C3L, p4, C3R, p1] twice, p6, [k2, p2] 3 times.

Row 9: [P2, k2] 3 times, p6, [p2, C3L, p2, C3R, p2] twice, p6, [k2, p2] 3 times.

Row 11: [P2, k2] 3 times, p6, [p3, C3L, C3R, p3] twice, p6, [k2, p2] 3 times.

Row 13: [P2, k2] 3 times, p6, [p4, C4B, p4] twice, p6, [k2, p2] 3 times.

Row 15: Work every st in patt as it presents.

Row 17: [P2, k2] 3 times, p6, [p4, C4B, p4] twice, p6, [k2, p2] 3 times.

Row 19: [P2, k2] 3 times, p6, [p3, C3R, C3L, p3] twice, p6, [k2, p2] 3 times.

Row 5: [P2, k2] 4 times, p6, [C3L, p6, C3R] twice, p6, [k2, p2] 4 times.

Row 7: [P2, k2] 4 times, p6, [p1, C3L, p4, C3R, p1] twice, p6, [k2, p2] 4 times.

Row 9: [P2, k2] 4 times, p6, [p2, C3L, p2, C3R, p2] twice, p6, [k2, p2] 4 times.

Row 11: [P2, k2] 4 times, p6, [p3, C3L, C3R, p3] twice, p6, [k2, p2] 4 times.

Row 13: [P2, k2] 4 times, p6, [p4, C4B, p4] twice, p6, [k2, p2] 4 times.

Row 15: Work every st in patt as it presents.

Row 17: [P2, k2] 4 times, p6, [p4, C4B, p4] twice, p6, [k2, p2] 4 times.

Row 19: [P2, k2] 4 times, p6, [p3, C3R, C3L, p3] twice, p6, [k2, p2] 4 times.

Row 21: [P2, k2] 4 times, p6, [p2, C3R, p2, C3L, p2] twice, p6, [k2, p2] 4 times.

Row 23: [P2, k2] 4 times, p6, [p1, C3R, p4, C3L, p1] twice, p6, [k2, p2] 4 times.

Row 21: [P2, k2] 3 times, p6, [p2, C3R, p2, C3L, p2] twice, p6, [k2, p2] 3 times.

Row 23: [P2, k2] 3 times, p6, [p1, C3R, p4, C3L, p1] twice, p6, [k2, p2] 3 times.

Row 25: [P2, k2] 3 times, p6, [C3R, p6, C3L] twice, p6, [k2, p2] 3 times.

Row 27: [P2, k2] 3 times, p6, k2, p8, C4F, p8, k2, p6, [k2, p2] 3 times.

Row 28: Work every st in patt as it presents.

Rep rows 1–28.

Rep rows 1–16.

Bind (cast) off.

Rib edging (make 2)

Cast on 10 sts.

Row 1: [K2, p2] twice, k2.

Row 2: [P2, k2] twice, p2.

Rows 3–250, or until work measure approx. 102in (260cm): Rep rows 1–2. Bind (cast) off.

To make up

- Weave in all loose ends.
- Wash the knit vigorously by hand, until it is felted to the desired degree (see page 124). Leave to dry.
- For seat cushion. Lay large knit panel on top of cushion, allowing enough to fold down over front gusset. Use one strip of the rib edging to make gusset for other three sides, sewing it to edge of knitted panel using knitting yarn. Cut canvas to size for base of cushion and sew in place using a sewing machine, or by hand using backstitch.
- Insert cushion pad and sew open side closed.
- For seat back. Stitch edging around all four sides of one knit panel, then attach other knit panel around three sides using knitting yarn, leaving one side open to slip in cushion pad.
- Insert cushion and sew closed using mattress stitch.

→ **CHANGING SIZES**

If your cushion is wider or narrower than the measurements given below, increase or decrease the number of rib stitches down either side. See also page 125.

Knitted blocks

Foam cubes covered in colorful knit create fun toys for stacking and knocking over. I've made this in a simple stockinette (stocking) stitch knit so it is a great project for a beginner knitter.

38

Skill level ★

Size
4 x 4in (10 x 10cm)

Materials
Yarn
Double knit yarn such as Baby Merino Silk DK from Rowan—66% merino, 34% tussah silk; approx. 147yds (135m) per 1¾oz (50g) ball

- Limone—approx. 1oz (30g)/88yds (80m)
- Bluebird—approx. 1oz (30g)/88yds (80m)
- Teal—approx. 1oz (30g)/88yds (80m)
- Straw—approx. 1oz (30g)/88yds (80m)
- Opal—approx. 1oz (30g)/88yds (80m)

Needles
Pair of US 6 (4mm) knitting needles

Other materials
- Knitter's sewing needle
- Five foam blocks, each measuring 4 x 4in (10 x 10cm)

Gauge (tension)
21 sts and 27 rows to 4in (10cm) over st st using US 6 (4mm) needles

Abbreviations
See page 126

Pattern
Main piece
Cast on 20 sts.
Beg with a k row, work 27 rows in st st.
Row 28 (ridge row): Knit.
Rep rows 1–28, 3 more times.
Bind (cast) off.

First side
Pick up 20 sts evenly spread on left-hand edge between rows 29 and 56. Beg with a k row, work 28 rows in st st. Bind (cast) off.

Second side
Work as for First Side, but on right-hand edge.

To make up
- Weave in loose ends.
- Press following instructions on the yarn band.
- Using mattress stitch, close seams around foam block.

Simplest bootees

These bootees are super-simple to knit, and as a set with the newborn mittens (see page 12), or cute cable hat (see page 10), would make a wonderful gift. They're ideal to keep precious little toes warm!

Skill level ★

Size
Newborn: 3½ x 2in (9 x 5cm)
3–6 months: 4 x 2⅜oz (10 x 6cm)

Materials
Yarn
Double knit yarn such as Baby Merino Silk DK from Rowan—66% merino, 34% tussah silk; approx. 147yds (135m) per 1¾oz (50g) ball
- Teal (A)—approx. 1oz (30g)/88yds (80m)
- Bluebird (B)—approx. ¼oz (14g)/ 44yds (40m)

OR
- Shell Pink (A)—approx. 1oz (30g)/ 88yds (80m)
- Rose (B)—approx. ½oz (14g)/44yds (40m)

NOTE: Use two ends of yarn held together throughout

Needles
Pair of US 7 (4.5mm) knitting needles

Other materials
- Knitter's sewing needle

Gauge (tension)
16 sts and 24 rows to 4in (10cm) over st st using US 7 (4.5mm) needles and two ends of yarn held together

Abbreviations
See page 126

Pattern
Top
Using A, cast on 36(40) sts.
Knit 11(13) rows.
Bind (cast) off.

Base
Using B, cast on 2(4) sts.
Row 1 and every alt row: Purl.

Row 26: K2, [p2, k2] to end.

Row 27: P2, [k2, p2] to end.

Rows 28–35: Rep rows 26–27, 4 times more.

Bind (cast) off in rib.

Left-hand piece

As for Right-hand Piece, but along left-hand edge.

To make up

- Weave in loose ends.
- Steam following instructions on the yarn band.

- Using mattress stitch, sew up the four corner seams.
- Using knitter's sewing needle, thread elastic through the knitting around the top edge on WS of rib.
- Slip the cover into the wicker basket and pull rib over outer edge, tighten elastic and secure.

Row 29: P8, C6F, p16.

Row 30: K16, p6, k8.

Rows 31–34: Rep rows 11–12 twice more.

Row 35: P8, k6, p16.

Change to B.

Beg with a p row, work 50 rows in st st.

Change to A.

Row 86: Purl.

Rows 87–110: Rep rows 11–34.

Rows 111–120: Rep rows 1–10.

Bind (cast) off in rib.

Right-hand piece

With RS facing and A, pick up 38 sts along right-hand edge of the rows worked in B.

Beg with a k row, work 25 rows in rev st st.

→ TYING THE LINING

A clever way to keep the lining secured to the bottom of the basket is to thread ribbons through the corners of the knitting and then through the corners of the basket, and tie bows on the outside.

Owl doorstop

Here's a lovely little weighted doorstop with real character.
The simple seed (moss) stitch gives texture to suggest the
owl's feathers.

Skill level ★★

Size

5 x 8 in (13 x 20cm)

Materials

Yarn

Double knit yarn such as Juxton Flock Jacob Wool—100% wool:
approx. 119yds (110m) per 1¾oz (50g) ball—or LB Collection®
Baby Alpaca Yarn from Lion Brand Yarns—100% baby alpaca:
approx 146yds (133m) per 1¾oz (50g) ball

• Natural fleece—1¾oz (50g)/119yds (110m)—or fawn
heather—1¾oz (50g)/146yds (133m)

• Small amounts of yellow and white DK yarn for beak and eyes

Needles

Set of four US 6 (4mm) double-pointed knitting needles
Pair of US 6 (4mm) knitting needles

Other materials

• Knitter's sewing needle

• 15½ x 8¾in (38 x 22cm) strip and 5in (13cm) diameter
circle of black lining material

• 3½lb (1.5kg) dried lentils

• Scrap of tapestry yarn for embroidering eyes

Gauge (tension)

17 sts and 40 rows to 4in (10cm) over patt using US 6 (4mm) needles

Abbreviations

See page 126

Pattern

Body

Cast on 60 sts.

Evenly distribute sts over 3 double-pointed needles. Place a marker to denote end of round.

Round 1: [K1, p1] to end.

Round 2: [P1, k1] to end.

Rep rounds 1–2, 37 times more. 76 rows completed

Bind (cast) off.

Beak

Using yellow yarn and straight knitting needles, cast on 5 sts.

Beg with a k row, work 4 rows in st st.

Row 5 (RS): P2tog, p1, p2togtbl. *3 sts*

Work 2 rows st st.

Row 8: P3tog and fasten off.

Eye (make 2)

Using white yarn and straight knitting needles, cast on 4 sts.

Row 1 (WS): Inc, k to last st, inc. *6 sts*

Row 2 and every alt row: Purl.

Row 3: Inc, k to last st, inc. *8 sts*

Row 5: Inc, k to last st, inc. *10 sts*

Row 7 and foll 2 alt rows: Knit.

Row 13: K2togtbl, k6, k2tog. *8 sts*

Row 15: K2togtbl, k4, k2tog. *6 sts*

Row 17: K2togtbl, k2, k2tog. *4 sts*

Bind (cast) off.

To make up

- Weave in loose ends.
- Steam following instructions on the yarn band.
- Using a sewing machine or by hand using backstitch, and taking a ⅜in (1cm) seam allowance, join short edges of lining strip to form tube. Sew across top edge.
- Attach circular piece to other end of tube, leaving 2in (5cm) opening.
- Fill with 3 ½lb (1.5kg) of dried lentils to give the doorstop weight, and sew opening closed by hand.
- Join seam across top of knitted tube to give flat edge.
- Attach eyes and beak using image as guide. Using tapestry yarn, embroider closed eyes.
- Slip knitting over the filled lining bag and hand stitch to circular base fabric.

→ KNITTING IN THE ROUND

This doorstop uses knitting in the round, so if you haven't tried this before turn to the instructions on page 117.

Giant knitted rug

What a wonderful way to add chunky texture to your nursery! Made using super-thick felted yarn and giant knitting needles, this is a surprisingly quick project to make.

50

Skill level ★

Size

51in (130cm) in diameter

→ DOING THE KNITTING

This knitting gets very heavy, so it is easiest to sit on the floor so that the weight is supported rather than hanging from the needle.

Materials

Yarn

Felted wool yarn such as Dreadlock Wool from Texere—100% wool; approx. 175yds (160m) per 4lb 8oz (2kg) cone

• Ecru—approx. 7lb (3.2kg)/280yds (256m)

Needles

Pair of 1¾in (4.5cm) knitting needles (see Resources, page 127)

Other materials

• Bodkin

Gauge (tension)

3 sts and 4.5 rows to 4in (10cm) over garter stitch using 1¾in (4.5cm) needles

Abbreviations

See page 126

Pattern

Main piece

Cast on 18 sts.

Row 1: K3, turn.

Row 2 and every alt row: Knit to end.

Row 3: K6, turn.

Row 5: K9, turn.

Row 7: K12, turn.

Row 9: K15, turn.

Row 11: K18.

Row 12: K18.

Rep rows 1–12, 13 more times.

Bind (cast) off.

To make up

• Weave in all loose ends.
• Join cast-on and bound- (cast-) off edges to form circle. Draw center stitches together and tie off.
• Steam flat.

CHAPTER TWO

Toddler's Room

The playroom can never have enough storage, and there are projects here to help you be organized, as well as keep the room looking lovely at the same time. Colorful yarns and simple stitch patterns combine in cheerful decorations a toddler will love.

Toy box

Creating additional seating and a handy storage solution, this knitted toy box is practical as well as striking, and fun to make. It does require a lot of knitting, but is certainly worth the effort.

Skill level ★★★

Size

Approx. 20½in (52cm) wide x 18½in (47cm) deep x 16in (41cm) high

Materials

Yarn

Fine 4ply yarn such as Pura Lana Baruffa 4ply from Robert Todd—100% extrafine merino wool; approx. 186yds (170m) per 1¾oz (50g) ball

NOTE: use two ends of yarn held together throughout

• Sunshine—17½oz (500g)/1860yds (1700m)

Needles

Pair of US 7 (4.5 mm) knitting needles

Other materials

• Toy box measuring 20½in (52cm) wide x 18½in (47cm) deep x 16in (41cm) high

• Knitter's sewing needle
• Cable needle
• Strong matching sewing thread
• Sewing needle

Gauge (tension)

19 sts and 25 rows to 4in (10cm) over st st using US 7 (4.5mm) needles

Abbreviations

C6F—cable 6 forward: slip next 3 sts onto cable needle and hold at front of work, knit next 3 sts from left-hand needle, then knit 3 sts from cable needle

C3L—cable 3 left: slip next 2 sts onto cable needle and hold at front of work, purl next st from left-hand needle, then knit 2 sts from cable needle

C3R—cable 3 right: slip next st onto cable needle and hold at back of work, knit next 2 sts from left-hand needle, then purl st from cable needle

See also page 126

Pattern

Box lid (make 1)

Cast on 94 sts.

Row 1: P10, k2, p11, k6, p11, k2, p2, k6, p2, k2, p11, k6, p11, k2, p10.

Row 2 and every alt row: Work every st in patt as it presents.

Row 3: P10, k2, p11, k6, p11, k2, p2, k6, p2, k2, p11, k6, p11, k2, p10.

Row 5: P10, k2, p11,C6F, p11, k2, p2, C6F, p2, k2, p11, C6F, p11, k2, p10.

Row 7: P10, C3L, p10, k6, p10, C3R, p2, k6, p2, C3L, p10, k6, p10, C3R, p10.

Row 9: P11, C3L, p9, k6, p9, C3R, p3, k6, p3, C3L, p9, k6, p9, C3R, p11.

Row 11: P12, C3L, p8, k6, p8, C3R, p4, k6, p4, C3L, p8, k6, p8, C3R, p12.

Row 13: P13, C3L, p7, k6, p7, C3R, p5, k6, p5, C3L, p7, k6, p7, C3R, p13.

Row 15: P14, C3L, p6, C6F, p6, C3R, p6, C6F, p6, C3L, p6, C6F, p6, C3R, p14.

Row 17: P15, C3L, p5, k6, p5, C3R, p7, k6, p7, C3L, p5, k6, p5, C3R, p15.

Row 19: P16, C3L, p4, k6, p4, C3R, p8, k6, p8, C3L, p4, k6, p4, C3R, p16.

Row 21: P17, C3L, p3, k6, p3, C3R, p9, k6, p9, C3L, p3, k6, p3, C3R, p17.

Row 23: P18, C3L, p2, k6, p2, C3R, p10, k6, p10, C3L, p2, k6, p2, C3R, p18.

Row 25: P19, k2, p2, C6F, p2, k2, p11, C6F, p11, k2, p2, C6F, p2, k2, p19.

Row 27: P18, C3R, p2, k6, p2, C3L, p10, k6, p10, C3R, p2, k6, p2, C3L, p18.

Row 29: P17, C3R, p3, k6, p3, C3L, p9, k6, p9, C3R, p3, k6, p3, C3L, p17.

Row 31: P16, C3R, p4, k6, p4, C3L, p8, k6, p8, C3R, p4, k6, p4, C3L, p16.

Row 33: P15, C3R, p5, k6, p5, C3L, p7, k6, p7, C3R, p5, k6, p5, C3L, p15.

Row 35: P14, C3R, p6, C6F, p6, C3L, p6, C6F, p6, C3R, p6, C6F, p6, C3L, p14.

Row 37: P13, C3R, p7, k6, p7, C3L, p5, k6, p5, C3R, p7, k6, p7, C3L, p13.

Row 39: P12, C3R, p8, k6, p8, C3L, p4, k6, p4, C3R, p8, k6, p8, C3L, p12.

Row 41: P11, C3R, p9, k6, p9, C3L, p3, k6, p3, C3R, p9, k6, p9, C3L, p11.

Row 43: P10, C3R, p10, k6, p10, C3L, p2, k6, p2, C3R, p10, k6, p10, C3L, p10.

Row 44: Work every st in patt as it presents.

Rows 5–44 form patt.

Rows 45–124: Rep rows 5 to 44 twice.

Rows 125–128: Work rows 1–4 once.

Bind (cast) off.

Box front and back (both alike, make 2)

Cast on 78 sts.

Row 1: P7, k2, p6, k6, p6, k2, p7, k6, p7, k2, p6, k6, p6, k2, p7.

Row 2: Work every st in patt as it presents.

Rows 3–40: Rep rows 1–2.

Row 41: P6, C3R, p6, k6, p6, C3L, p6, k6, p6, C3R, p6, k6, p6, C3L, p6.

Row 43: P5, C3R, p7, k6, p7, C3L, p5, k6, p5, C3R, p7, k6, p7, C3L, p5.

Row 45: P4, C3R, p8, k6, p8, C3L, p4, k6, p4, C3R, p8, k6, p8, C3L, p4.

Row 47: P3, C3R, p9, k6, p9, C3L, p3, k6, p3, C3R, p9, k6, p9, C3L, p3.

Row 49: P2, C3R, p10, k6, p10, C3L, p2, k6, p2, C3R, p10, k6, p10, C3L, p2.

Row 51: P2, k2, p11, C6F, p11, k2, p2, C6F, p2, k2, p11, C6F, p11, k2, p2.

Row 53: P2, C3L, p10, k6, p10, C3R, p2, k6, p2, C3L, p10, k6, p10, C3R, p2.

Row 55: P3, C3L, p9, k6, p9, C3R, p3, k6, p3, C3L, p9, k6, p9, C3R, p3.

Row 57: P4, C3L, p8, k6, p8, C3R, p4, k6, p4, C3L, p8, k6, p8, C3R, p4.

Row 59: P5, C3L, p7, k6, p7, C3R, p5, k6, p5, C3L, p7, k6, p7, C3R, p5.

Row 61: P6, C3L, p6, C6F, p6, C3R, p6, C6F, p6, C3L, p6, C6F, p6, C3R, p6.

Row 63: P7, C3L, p5, k6, p5, C3R, p7, k6, p7, C3L, p5, k6, p5, C3R, p7.

Row 65: P8, C3L, p4, k6, p4, C3R, p8, k6, p8, C3L, p4, k6, p4, C3R, p8.

Row 67: P9, C3L, p3, k6, p3, C3R, p9, k6, p9, C3L, p3, k6, p3, C3R, p9.

Row 69: P10, C3L, p2, k6, p2, C3R, p10, k6, p10, C3L, p2, k6, p2, C3R, p10.

Row 71: P11, k2, p2, C6F, p2, k2, p11, C6F, p11, k2, p2, C6F, p2, k2, p11.

Row 72: Work every st in patt as it presents.

Rows 73–80: As rows 41–48.

Bind (cast) off.

Box sides (both alike, make 2)

Cast on 60 sts.

Beg with a RS p row, work 80 rows in rev st st.

Bind (cast) off.

To make up

- Weave in loose ends.
- Steam following instructions on the yarn band.
- Stretch knit for box lid over the existing cover of toy box and using staple gun secure on inside.
- Using mattress stitch, join side seams of back, front, and side panels, them slip onto base of toy box and staple under and inside box.

Cozy lampshade

A chunky Aran pattern on this shade gives a really snug feel to the room. The light picks up the fine fibers of the mohair in the yarn to create a soft glow.

Skill level ★★

Size

8in (20cm) high x 10in (25cm) diameter

Materials

Yarn

Chunky yarn such as Cocoon from Rowan—80% merino, 20% kid mohair: approx. 126yds (115m) per 3½oz (100g) ball

• Kiwi—approx. 5oz (140g)/180yds (160m)

Needles

Pair of size US 15 (10mm) knitting needles

Other materials

• Dome lampshade measuring approx. 8in (20cm) high x 10in (25cm) diameter
• Cable needle
• Knitter's sewing needle
• Elastic cord in color to match yarn

Gauge (tension)

24 sts to 9in (23cm) and 20 rows to 7in (18cm) over cable patt using US 15 (10mm) needles

Abbreviations

C4B—cable 4 back: slip next 2 sts onto cable needle and hold at back of work, knit next 2 sts from left-hand needle, then knit 2 sts from cable needle

C4F—cable 4 front: slip next 2 sts onto cable needle and hold at front of work, knit next 2 sts from left-hand needle, then knit 2 sts from cable needle

C3L—cable 3 left: slip next 2 sts onto cable needle and hold at front of work, purl next st from left-hand needle, then knit 2 sts from cable needle

C3R—cable 3 right: slip next st onto cable needle and hold at back of work, knit next 2 sts from left-hand needle, then purl st from cable needle

See also page 126

Pattern

Main piece

Cast on 24 sts.

Row 1: P4, k2, p4, k4, p4, k2, p4.

Row 2: Work every st in patt as it presents to last 4 sts, turn.

Row 3: K2, p4, C4F, p4, k2, p4.

Row 4: Work every st in patt as it presents.

58

Row 5: P4, C3L, p2, C3R, C3L, p2, C3R, p4.

Row 6: Work every st in patt as it presents to last 5 sts, turn.

Row 7: C3L, C3R, p2, C3L, C3R, p5.

Row 8: Work every st in patt as it presents.

Row 9: P6, C4B, p4, C4B, p6.

Row 10: Work every st in patt as it presents to last 6 sts, turn.

Row 11: K4, p4, k4, p6.

Row 12: Work every st in patt as it presents.

Row 13: P6, C4B, p4, C4B, p6.

Row 14: Work every st in patt as it presents to last 5 sts, turn.

Row 15: C3R, C3L, p2, C3R, C3L, p5.

Row 16: Work every st in patt as it presents.

Row 17: P4, C3R, p2, C3L, C3R, p2, C3L, p4.

Row 18: Work every st in patt as it presents to last 4 sts, turn.

Row 19: K2, p4, C4F, p4, k2, p4.

Row 20: Work every st in patt as it presents.

Rep rows 1–20, 3 more times.

Bind (cast) off.

To make up
- Weave in all loose ends.
- Sew together the cast-on and bound-(cast-) off rows.
- Using knitter's sewing needle, thread elastic through the knitting around the top and bottom of the knitted cover.
- Slip the cover over the shade and pull the elastic tight so that the cover perfectly fits the shade. Knot the ends of the elastic and trim short.

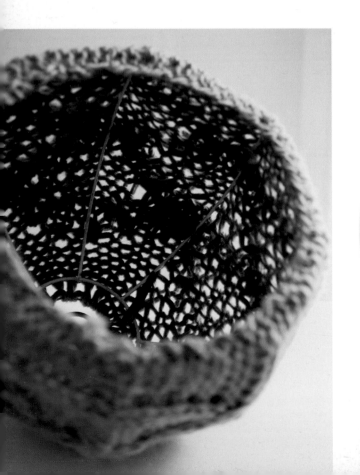

→ **CHOOSING A SHADE**

Vintage lampshades are easy to find in thrift stores, and this knitting will fit over a shade that is slightly larger or smaller than the one used here.

- Fill the bathtub with the hottest tap water possible and put in as much washing detergent as for a normal single load in a washing machine. Lay the bundles in the hot water. Wearing the rubber boots, climb into the bath and stomp on the bundles for about five minutes to encourage a certain amount of felting. Drain the bath, then rinse the bundles several times with cold water to remove any trace of detergent.
- Spin the bundles dry if you have a washing machine, or squeeze them until you have removed as much water as possible if you do not. Open the bundles and lay the now slightly felted wool on a drying rack for at least 12 hours to dry. Rep until you have felted both bags of roving.
- Once the wool is fully dry, pull the end of one length apart so that the roving is split evenly into two: as you gently pull, the roving should easily split down the entire length. Rep this on each split length so that the original length is now split into four. Ball up your newly created yarn.

Pattern

Main piece

Cast on 7 sts.

Row 1: Inc in every st. *14 sts*

Row 2: Knit.

Row 3: Inc in every st. *28 sts*

Row 4: Knit.

Row 5: [K1, inc] to end. *42 sts*

Rows 6–20: Knit

Bind (cast) off.

To make up

- Using the bodkin, weave in all the loose ends.
- Using the same yarn, lace up the side seam and draw base closed.

→ MAKING THE YARN

Try to split the roving as evenly as possible, but don't worry if it is not all exactly the same—irregularities will just add to the lovely texture.

Pig pillow

Every child will love this character pillow. Instead of knitting in intarsia, which would give a flat finish, I've designed this in layers to create details in relief.

Skill level ★★

Size

16 x 16in (40 x 40cm)

Materials

Wool yarn such as Chunky Wool from Texere—100% pure wool; approx. 120yds (110m) per 3½oz (100g) ball

- Ecru (A) approx.—4½oz (130g)/155yds (145m)
- Pink (B)—2¾oz (75g)/95yds (85m)
- Slate (C)—¾oz (10g)/10yds (10m)

Needles

Pair of US 10 (6mm) knitting needles

Other materials

- 16 x 16in (40 x 40cm) pillow pad
- Small amount of toy stuffing
- Fabric measuring 17 x 17in (43 x 43cm) for cushion back
- Stitch holder
- Knitter's sewing needle
- Sewing needle and ecru sewing thread

Gauge (tension)

13 sts and 20 rows to 4in (10cm) over st st using US 10 (6mm) needles

Abbreviations

See page 126

Pattern

Base

Using A, cast on 56 sts.
Beg with a k row, work 86 rows in st st.
Bind (cast) off.

Pig face

Using B, cast on 15 sts.
Row 1 (WS): Inc, k to last st, inc. *17 sts*
Row 2: Inc, p to last st, inc. *19 sts*
Rows 3–10: Rep rows 1–2, 4 times. *35 sts*
Row 11: Knit.
Row 12: Inc, p to last st, inc. *37 sts*

Rows 13–16: Rep rows 11–12, twice. *41 sts*
Row 17: Knit.
Row 18: Purl.
Row 19: Knit.
Row 20: Inc, p to last st, inc. *43 sts*
Rows 21–32: Work in st st.
Row 33: K2togtbl, k to last 2 sts, k2tog. *41 sts*
Row 34: Purl.
Row 35: Knit.
Row 36: Purl.
Row 37: K2togtbl, k to last 2 sts, k2tog. *39 sts*
Rows 38–43: Rep rows 36–37, 3 times. *33 sts*
Row 44: P2tog, p to last 2 sts, p2togtbl. *31 sts*
Row 45: K2togtbl, k to last 2 sts, k2tog. *29 sts*
Rows 46–47: Rep rows 44 and 45. *25 sts*
Row 48: P2tog, p to last 2 sts, p2tog tbl. *23 sts*

Row 49: Cast on 6 sts at beginning of row, knit 12 sts, slip rem 17 sts onto stitch holder.

First ear

Cont on 12 sts on needle.

Row 50: Purl.

Row 51: Knit.

Row 52: Purl.

Row 53: K2togtbl, k to last 2 sts, k2tog. *10 sts*

Rep rows 50–53 once more. *8 sts*

Row 58: Purl.

Row 59: K2togtbl, k4, k2tog. *6 sts*

Row 60: Purl.

Row 61: K2togtbl, k2, k2tog. *4 sts*
Bind (cast) off.

Second ear

With WS facing, transfer stitches from holder onto US 6 (4mm) needle so that point of needle is in center of knitting. Rejoin yarn.

Row 49 (WS): Bind (cast) off first 11 sts, knit to end of row. *6 sts*

Row 50: Cast on 6 sts at beg of row and p to end. *12 sts*

Row 51: Knit.

Row 52: Purl.

Row 53: K2togtbl, k to last 2 sts, k2tog. *10 sts*

Row 54: Purl.

Rep rows 51–54 once more. *8 sts*

Row 59: K2togtbl, k4, k2tog. *6 sts*

Row 60: Purl.

Row 61: K2togtbl, k2, k2tog. *4 sts*
Bind (cast) off.

Snout

Using B, cast on 36 sts.

Row 1 (RS): Knit.

Rows 2–6: Work in st st.

Row 7: Purl.

Row 8: [K2tog, k1] to end. *24 sts*

Row 9: [P4, p2tog] to end. *20 sts*

Row 10: [K3, k2tog] to end. *16 sts*

Row 11: [P2, p2tog] to end. *12 sts*

Row 12: [K1, k2tog] to end. *8 sts*

Cut yarn and thread through rem 8 sts and secure.

Eye (make 2)

Using A, cast on 4 sts.

Row 1 and foll 3 alt rows (WS): Purl.

Row 2: Inc, k2, inc. *6 sts*

Row 4: Inc, k4, inc. *8 sts*

Row 6: Knit.

Row 8: Knit.

Row 9: P2tog, p4, p2togtbl. *6 sts*

Row 10: K2togtbl, k2, k2tog. *4 sts*
Bind (cast) off.

To make up

- Weave in all loose ends. Press pieces with steam iron.
- With knitting yarn, sew bottom edge of ears to top of face.
- With knitting yarn, join short ends of snout, then sew snout to center of face, leaving small gap for stuffing.
- With knitting yarn, sew eyes on face.
- With knitting yarn, sew face to cushion front, leaving small gap for stuffing.
- Wash gently and allow to dry.
- Stuff snout and sew closed.
- Stuff head lightly and sew closed.
- With C, embroider mouth and eyes as in photograph.
- With right sides together, sew fabric square to knitted base, taking ⅝in (1.5cm) seam allowances and leaving one side open. Turn RS out, insert pillow pad, then sew open side closed.

65

→ STUFFING THE PIG

I have put stuffing between the pig face and the cushion base, which adds an extra impact, but you can leave the face flat if you prefer.

Trellis blanket

Add color and pattern to your child's room with this sumptuously soft throw; use it as a bed runner so it is easily available to snuggle up in. Although I've gone for turquoise shades, you could make the blanket in pink tones for a little girl's room.

Skill level ★★★

Size
Approx. 45 x 29in (114 x 74cm)

Materials

Yarn
Chunky yarn such as Cocoon from Rowan—80% merino, 20% kid mohair: approx. 126yds (115m) per 3½ oz (100g) ball

- Seascape (A)—approx. 17½ oz (500g)/630yds (575m)
- Duck Down (B)—approx. 5¾ oz (160g)/210yds (185m)

Needles
Pair of US 10½ (6.5mm) knitting needles

Other materials
- Knitter's sewing needle

Gauge (tension)
18 sts (3 patt reps) and 32 rows (4 patt reps) to 4¾ in (12cm) over patt using US 10½ (6.5mm) needles

Abbreviations
See page 126

Note: Slip sts purlwise with yarn at back unless otherwise instructed

Pattern

Main piece
Using A, cast on 111 sts.
Beg with a p row, work 4 rows in st st.
Change to B.
Row 5 (WS): K1, [slip 3 purlwise, p1, slip 2 purlwise] to last 2 sts, slip 1 purlwise, k1.
Change to A.
Row 6: Knit.
Row 7: Purl.
Change to B.
Row 8: K1, [pick up the strand 3 rows below the next st and knit this and the next st together, slip 5 purlwise] to last 2 sts, pick up the strand 3 rows below the next st and knit this and the next st together, k1.
Row 9: K1, sl1 purlwise with yarn in front, [slip 5 purlwise with yarn at back, slip 1 purlwise with yarn in front] to last st, k1.
Change to A.
Row 10: Knit.
Row 11: Purl.
Change to B.
Row 12: K1, [slip 3 purlwise, pick up the strand 3 rows below the next st and knit this and the next st together, slip 2 purlwise] to last 2 sts, slip 1 purlwise, k1.
Row 13: K1, [sl3 purlwise with yarn at back, slip 1 purlwise with yarn in front, slip 2 purlwise with yarn at back] to last 2 sts, slip 1 purlwise with yarn at back, k1.
Change to A.
Rep rows 6–13, 35 more times, then rep rows 6–12 once more.
Change to A.

Row 7: P3, [p1, C3L, p4, C3R, p1] twice, p3.

Row 9: P3, [p2, C3L, p2, C3R, p2] twice, p3.

Row 11: P3, [p3, C3L, C3R, p3] twice, p3.

Row 13: P3, [p4, C4B, p4] twice, p3.

Row 15: Work every st in patt as it presents.

Row 17: P3, [p4, C4B, p4] twice, p3.

Row 19: P3, [p3, C3R, C3L, p3] twice, p3.

Row 21: P3, [p2, C3R, p2, C3L, p2] twice, p3.

Row 23: P3, [p1, C3R, p4, C3L, p1], twice, p3.

Row 25: P3, [C3R, p6, C3L] twice, p3.

Row 27: P3, k2, p8, C4F, p8, k2, p3.

Row 28: Work every st in patt as it presents.

Rep rows 1–28 twice more.

Bind (cast) off.

Rib trim

Work right-hand and left-hand rib trims as for First Shelf.

To make up

- Weave in all loose ends.
- Steam flat and shape into a rectangle.
- Sew the cast-on edge to the bound-(cast-) off edge to form a knitted tube.
- Slip tube over shelf before assembling the shelving unit.
- If the shelves are already assembled, you will need to sew the tube closed around the shelf.

Cat coat hanger

This feline coat hanger might just be too cute to hang in the wardrobe! Instead, use to display your child's favorite outfit. You could even fill the head with lavender.

Skill level ★★

Size

Approx. 17in (43cm)

Materials

Yarn

Chunky yarn such as Chunky Wool from Texere —100% pure new wool; approx. 120 yds (110m) per 3½oz (100g) ball
• Slate (A)—approx. ¾oz (20g)/25yds (20m)

Double knit yarn such as Baby Merino Silk DK from Rowan—66% merino, 34% tussah silk; approx. 147yds (135m) per 1¾oz (50g) ball
• Rose (B)—approx. ¾oz (20g)/65yds (55m)

Needles

Pair each of US 7 (4.5mm) and US 3 (3.25mm) knitting needles

Other materials

• Knitter's sewing needle
• 16in (40cm) wooden coat hanger
• 2 buttons for eyes
• Tapestry yarn for whiskers
• Toy stuffing

Gauge (tension)

24 sts and 32 rows to 4in (10cm) over st st using Baby Merino Silk and US 3 (3.25mm) needles

Abbreviations

See page 126

Pattern

Head

Using US 7 (4.5mm) needles and A, cast on 8 sts.
Work in rev st st.
Row 1 and every alt row (RS): Purl.
Row 2: Inc in every st. *16 sts*
Row 4: [Inc, k3] to end. *20 sts*

Row 6: Inc in every st. *40 sts*
Row 8: Knit.
Row 10: Knit.
Row 12: Knit.
Row 14: [K2tog] to end. *20 sts*
Row 16: [K2tog, k3] to end. *16 sts*
Row 18: [K2tog] to end. *8 sts*
Row 19: [P2tog], to end. *4 sts*

Cut yarn, leaving a long end, and thread through rem sts, draw tight to close nose end of head. Do not fasten off.

Outer ears (make 2)

Using US 7 (4.5mm) needles and A, cast on 4 sts.
Row 1: Purl.
Row 2: Knit.
Row 3: Purl.
Row 4: K2togtbl, k2tog.
Bind (cast) off.

Inner ears (make 2)

Using US 3 (3.25mm) needles and B, cast on 4 sts.

Row 1: Purl.

Row 2: Knit.

Row 3: Purl.

Row 4: K2togtbl, k2tog.

Bind (cast) off.

Paws (make 2)

Using US p (4.5mm) needles and A, cast on 11 sts.

Beg with a k row, work 10 rows in rev st st.

Bind (cast) off.

Hanger

Using US 3 (3.25mm) needles and B, cast on 16 sts.

Rows 1–2: [K2, p2] to end.

Rows 3–4: [P2, k2] to end.

Rep rows 1–4, 26 more times.

Bind (cast) off.

To make up

- Weave in all loose ends.
- Wrap hanger cover round coat hanger, slipping hook through knitting, and join on underside with knitting yarn and mattress stitch.
- Fold paws in half and sew side seams and cast-on edge.
- Stitch paw on each end of hanger.

- For head, using attached long end, join row ends. Fill with toy stuffing then gather cast-on edge to close head.
- Sew inner ears to front of outer ears and sew to head in position.
- Sew buttons on for eyes.
- Using photograph as a guide, embroider nose and mouth in B.
- Thread hook of coat hanger through back of head.
- Secure lower edge of head to hanger by using A and stitching around the hanger.

→ HANGER SIZE

This pattern is for a standard 16in (40cm) coat hanger, but you can easily reduce the length of the hanger piece to make it fit a smaller version.

Vintage children's chair

Update a cute retro chair with a colorful cover knitted to match your nursery. Inspired by the bespoke furniture from my collection, this unique piece would also look stylish in neutral colors.

Skill level ★★

Size

23½in (60cm) high by 13¾in (35cm) deep by 13in (33cm) wide

Can be adjusted to fit your own chair (see page 125)

Materials

Yarn

Wool yarn such as Chunky Wool from Texere—100% pure wool; approx. 120yds (110m) per 3½oz (100g) ball

Quantities will depend on individual chair measurements, but as a guide:

- Cerise (A)—7oz (200g)/240yds (220m)
- Turquoise (B)—1½oz (40g)/52yds (44m)

Needles

Pair of US 10 (6mm) knitting needles

Other materials

- ¼in (5mm) thick foam to cover chair seat and back if they are not already cushioned
- Staple gun
- Black fabric to cover underside of chair seat
- Knitter's sewing needle

Gauge (tension)

12 sts and 20 rows to 4in (10cm) over st st using US 10 (6mm) needles

Abbreviations

LT—left twist: skip the next st to be knitted and knit into the back loop of the second st, knit into the back loops of both sts (the st you skipped and the second st, slip both sts from left-hand needle

RT—right twist: k2tog and leave sts on left-hand needle, knit the first of these two sts again, slip both sts from left-hand needle

See also page 126

Pattern

Chair back

*Using A, cast on 34 stitches.

Row 1 and every alt row: Purl.

Row 2 (RS): K1, [LT, k4, RT] to last st, k1.

Row 4: K2, [LT, k2, RT, k2] to end.

Row 6: K3, [LT, RT, k4] to last 7 sts, LT, RT, k3.

Row 8: K4, [RT, k6] to last 6 sts, RT, k4.

Row 10: K3, [RT, LT, k4] to last 7 sts, RT, LT, k3.

Row 12: K2, [RT, k2, LT, k2] to end.

Row 14: K1, [RT, k4, LT] to last st, k1.

Row 16: K8, [LT, k6] to last 2 sts, k2.*

Rows 17–64: Rep rows 1–16, 3 more times.

Bind (cast) off.

Chair seat

Work as for Chair Back from * to *.

Mark each end of last row with contrast thread.

Rep rows 1–16, 4 more times.

Mark each end of last row with contrast thread.

Rep rows 1–16 twice more.

Bind (cast) off.

**Using B, pick up 50 sts along right-hand side edge between markers.

Row 1: P2, [k2, p2] to end.

Row 1: K2, [p2, k2] to end.

Rows 3–18: Rep rows 1–2, 8 times more.

Bind (cast) off.**

Rep ** to ** along left-hand side edge.

To make up

- Weave in all loose ends.
- Wash the pieces vigorously by hand, until it is felted to the desired degree (see page 124). Leave to dry.
- Cover the seat and back with thin foam to add softness (if your chair is already cushioned you will not need to do this).
- Wrap the chair back piece around the frame to fully encase the chair back and secure with mattress stitch (see page 119).
- Stretch the knit over the chair seat and secure underneath with staple gun.
- Cover the underneath of the seat with black fabric, turning under the edges of the fabric and overlapping the edges of the knitting; staple gun the fabric in place.

→ MEASURING YOUR CHAIR

As your chair is likely to be a different size to this one, follow the instructions on page 125 to measure your own chair and adjust the pattern to fit it.

Knitted love letters

Make a heartfelt decoration with this knitted letter wall art.
These pop colors are perfect for a nursery that's been decorated
in a neutral scheme.

Skill level ★

Size
Each letter measures approx. 8½ x 6in (22 x 15cm)

Materials
Yarn

Wool yarn such as Chunky Wool from Texere—100%
pure new wool; approx. 120 yds (110m) per 3½ oz
(100g) ball
- Pink (A)—3½ oz (100g)/ 120 yds (110m)
- Cerise (B)—1¾ oz (50g)/ 60 yds (55m)
- Turquoise (C)—1¾ oz (50g)/ 60 yds (55m)

Needles
Pair of US 9 (5.5mm) knitting needles
Set of four US 9 (5.5mm) double-pointed needles

Other materials
- Cardboard letters for L, O, V, E (see Resources on
  page 127)
- Fabric for back of letters, cut ¼ in (5mm) larger than
  letters all around
- Stitch holder

- Knitter's sewing needle
- Matching sewing thread
- Sewing needle

Gauge (tension)
13 sts and 18 rows to 4in (10cm) over st st using US 9
(5.5mm) needles

Abbreviations
See page 126

Pattern
Letter L

Using A and straight needles,
cast on 12 sts.

Beg with a k row, work 15 rows
in st st.

Row 16: P11, turn.

Row 17 and every alt row: Knit.

Row 18: P10, turn.

Row 20: P9, turn.

Row 22: P8, turn.

Row 24: P7, turn.

Row 26: P6, turn.

→ PAINTING THE LETTERS

Paint the cardboard letters
in colors to match the yarns
for a perfect finish.

Row 28: P5, turn.

Row 30: P4, turn.

Row 32: P3, turn.

Row 34: P4, turn.

Row 36: P5, turn.

Row 38: P6, turn.

Row 40: P7, turn.

Row 42: P8, turn.

Row 44: P9, turn.

Row 46: P10, turn.

Row 48: P11, turn.

Rows 49–80: Work in st st.

Bind (cast) off.

Letter ends (make 2)

Using A and straight needles, cast on 5 sts.

Beg with a k row, work 5 rows in st st.

Bind (cast) off.

Letter O

Using B and double-pointed needles, cast on 60 sts.

Evenly distribute sts over 3 double-pointed needles. Place a marker to denote end of round.

Rounds 1–5: Knit.

Round 6: K4, inc, k20, inc, k8, inc, k20, inc, k4. *64 sts*

Round 7: Knit.

Round 8: K5, inc, k21, inc, k9, inc, k21, inc, k4. *68 sts*

Round 9: Knit.

Round 10: K6, inc, k22, inc, k10, inc, k22, inc, k4. *72 sts*

Rounds 11–17: Knit.

Bind (cast) off.

Letter V

Using C and straight needles, cast on 13 sts.

Row 1: Knit.

Row 2 and every alt row: Purl.

Row 3: Knit.

Row 5: K6, m1, k1, m1, k6. *15 sts*

Row 7: Knit.

Row 9: K7, m1, k1, m1, k7. *17 sts*

Row 11: Knit.

Row 13: K8, m1, k1, m1, k8. *19 sts*

Row 15: K9, k1 in back of loop of stitch below next st then k next st, k9. *20 sts*

Row 17: K10, slip rem stitches onto a stitch holder, turn and cont on 10 sts on needle.

Row 18: Cast on 3 sts at center edge, p13. *13 sts*

Work 21 rows in st st. Row 39 completed.

Bind (cast) off.

Slip sts on holder onto needle.

Row 17. Cast on 3 sts at center edge, k13. *13 sts*

Work 22 rows in st st. *Row 39 completed*

Bind (cast) off.

Letter ends (make 3)

Using C and straight needles, cast on 5 sts.

Beg with a k row, work 5 rows in st st.

Bind (cast) off.

Letter E

Follow rows 1–69 of Letter L.

Row 70: P11, turn.

Row 71 and every alt row: Knit.

Row 72: P10, turn

Row 74: P9, turn.

Row 76: P8, turn.

Row 78: P7, turn.

Row 80: P6, turn.

Row 82: P5, turn.

Row 84: P4, turn.

Row 86: P3, turn.

Row 88: P4, turn.

Row 90: P5, turn.

Row 92: P6, turn.

Row 94: P7, turn.

Row 96: P8, turn.

Row 98: P9, turn.

Row 100: P10, turn.

Row 102: P11, turn.

Rows 103–117: Work in st st.

Bind (cast) off.

Pick up 6 sts along right-hand edge in center of knitted piece.

Row 1: Cast on 3 sts, p9.

Row 2: Cast on 3 sts, k12.

Rows 3–13: Work in st st.

Bind (cast) off.

Letter ends (make 3)

Using A and straight needles, cast on 5 sts.

Beg with a k row, work 5 rows in st st.

Bind (cast) off.

To make up

- Weave in all loose ends.
- Wash the knitting by hand, slightly felting it (see page 124).
- Paint letters in colors to match knitting (optional).
- Wrap each letter in the knit and draw together on back.
- Cover back seam with fabric and stitch neatly in place.
- Sew letter ends on L, V, and E.
- Create small loop from knitting yarn at top of each letter to hang it by.

Textured knit pinboards

Create a set of beautiful pinboards that can be used to display notes or pictures, or why not embroider one with your little one's initial? They're also lovely enough to be left bare. Mix and match a few in varying colors and knit patterns.

Skill level ★★★

Size

5in (13cm), 7in (18cm), or 12in (31cm)

Materials

Yarn

DK-weight yarn such as Snuggly Baby Bamboo from Sirdar—80% bamboo, 20% wool; approx. 104yds (95m) per 1¾oz (50g) ball

- Dexter Blue (A)—approx. ½oz (15g)/30yds (30m)
- Putty (B)—approx. 1oz (30g)/60yds (60m)
- Flip Flop (C)—approx. 1½oz (42g)/90yds (80m)

Needles

Set of five US 9 (5.5mm) double-pointed knitting needles
Pair each of US 9 (5.5mm) and US 5 (3.75mm) knitting needles

Other materials

- Embroidery hoops in 5in (13cm), 7in (18cm), and 12in (31cm)
- Cable needle

- Complementary fabric for appliqué
- Fusible interfacing
- Sewing needle and sewing thread to match fabric

Gauge (tension)

All three pinboards are based on a standard stockinette (stocking) stitch gauge (tension) of 22 sts and 28 rows to 4in (10cm) using US 6 (4mm) needles

Abbreviations

C4Finc2—cable 4 front increase 2 stitches: slip next 2 sts onto cable needle and hold at front of work, knit next 2 sts from left-hand needle, make 2 sts, then knit 2 sts from cable needle
C6Finc2—cable 6 front increase 2 sts: slip next 3 sts onto cable needle and hold at front of work, knit next 3 sts from left-hand needle, make 2 sts, then knit 3 sts from cable needle
See also page 126

Pattern

5in (13cm) pinboard
Using US 9 (5.5mm) double-pointed needles and A, cast on 8 sts.

Rounds 1–2: [K1, m1] to end.

16 sts–32 sts

Round 3: Knit

Round 4: [K4, m1p] to end. *40 sts*

Round 5: [K4, p1] to end.

Round 6: [K4, m1p, p1, m1p] to end.

56 sts

Round 7: [K4, p3] to end.

Round 8: [C4F, p3] to end.

Round 9: [K4, p3] to end.

Round 10: [K4, m1p, p3, m1p] to end.

72 sts

Rounds 11–13: [K4, p5] to end.

Round 14: [K4, m1p, p5, m1p] to end.

88 sts

Rounds 15–17: [K4, p7] to end.

Round 18: [C4F inc2, p7] to end.

104 sts

Rounds 19–21: [K6, p7] to end.

Round 22: [K6, m1p, p7, m1p] to end.

120 sts

Rounds 23–25: [K6, p9] to end.

Round 26: [K6, m1p, p9, m1p] to end.

136 sts

Round 27: [K6, p11] to end.

Round 28: [C6F, p11] to end.

Round 29: [K6, p11] to end.

Round 30: [K6, m1p, p11, m1p] to end.

152 sts

Rounds 31–33: [K6, p13] to end.

Round 34: [K6, m1p, p13, m1p] to end.

168 sts

Rounds 35–37: [K6, p15] to end.

Round 38: [C6F inc2, p15] to end.
184 sts

Rounds 39–41: [K8, p15] to end.

Round 42: [K8, m1p, p15, m1p] to end.
200 sts

Rounds 43–45: [K8, p17] to end.
Bind (cast) off.

Pouffe sides

Using straight needles and B, cast on
76 sts.

Row 1: [K2, p2] to end.

Rep row 1 until all yarn is used.

Change to C.

Rep row 1 until all yarn is used.

Bind (cast) off.

To make up

- Weave in all loose ends.
- Wash the knitting vigorously by hand
  to felt it (see page 124), until top circle
  measures 18 ½ in (47cm) diameter
  and side strip measures 56 x 18 ½ in
  (142 x 47cm). Leave to dry.
- Make drum-shaped inner pad by
  cutting the light-colored fabric into two
  circles 18 ½ in (47cm) in diameter and
  a strip measuring 56 x 18 ½ in (142 x
  47cm). Taking a ⅜ in (1cm) seam
  allowance throughout, sew the short
  ends of the long strip right sides
  together to make a tube. With right
  sides together, sew the fabric circles
  to the top and bottom of the tube,
  leaving a 4in (10cm) gap in one seam
  for filling.
- Turn right side out through the gap
  and fill with beanbag beads until firm.
  Sew the gap closed by hand.
- Make cover in felted knitting by sewing
  the short ends of the long strip right
  sides together to make a tube. With
  right sides together, sew the circle to
  the top of the tube.
- Slip the filled pad into the open end.
- Cut black fabric circle measuring
  18 ½ in (47cm) diameter, turn under
  edges all around and sew to bottom
  of knitted tube by hand.

→ **STITCH MARKER**

A loop of contrast color yarn works
just as well as a stitch marker to mark
the end of each round.

Row 36: Bind (cast) off 10 sts at start of row, k to end. *20 sts*

Row 37: K10, inc, k9. *21 sts*

Row 38: K1, k2togtbl, k6, inc, k1, inc, k6, k2tog, k1.

Row 39: K1, k2togtbl, k6, inc, k1, inc, k6, k2tog, k1.

Row 40: K1, k2togtbl, k7, inc, k7, k2tog, k1. *20 sts*

Row 41: K1, k2togtbl, k5, inc, k2, inc, k5, k2tog, k1.

Row 42–45: Knit.

Row 46: K1, inc, k16, inc, k1. *22 sts*

Rows 47–50: Knit.

Row 51: [K2tog] 11 times. *11 sts*

Row 52: Knit.

Row 53: K1, [k2tog] 5 times. *6 sts*

Row 54: [K2tog] 3 times. *3 sts*

Thread end through rem 3 sts and pull tight.

Gusset

Cast on 14 sts.

Row 1: Knit.

Row 2: Inc, k12, inc. *16 sts*

Row 3: Knit.

Row 4: k2togtbl, k12, k2tog. *14 sts*

Row 5: Knit

Bind (cast) off.

Chunky knit lamb

Made in an unusual, undyed roving yarn, this lovely, gentle lamb will swiftly become a firm favorite. A real lamb's tight curls of fleece are echoed in the garter stitch texture of this knitted version.

89

Skill level ★★

Size

Approx 12 x 7in (30 x 18cm)

Materials

Yarn

Lightly twisted wool, also known as a pencil roving, such Bella from Texere—100% pure wool: approx. 60yds (55m) per 3½ oz (100g) ball

- Ecru—approx. 4oz (113g)/80yds (75m)

Needles

Pair of US 10½ (6.5mm) knitting needles

Other materials

- Toy stuffing
- Knitter's sewing needle
- Strong matching sewing thread
- Sewing needle

Gauge (tension)

11 sts and 20 rows to 4in (10cm) over garter stitch using US 10½ (6.5mm) needles

Abbreviations

See page 126

Pattern

Body

Cast on 40 sts for back legs and rear end.

Rows 1–10: Knit.

Row 11: Bind (cast) off 10 sts, k20, bind (cast) off 10 sts and break yarn. Rejoin yarn to rem 20 sts.

Rows 12–24: Knit.

Row 25: Cast on 10 sts at start of row, k to end. *30 sts*

Row 26: Cast on 10 sts at start of row, k to end. *40 sts*

Rows 27–34: Knit.

Row 35: Bind (cast) off 10 sts at start of row, k to end. *30 sts*

and wrap more roving in the same way until you have prepared it all.

- Fill the bathtub with the hottest tap water possible and put in as much washing detergent as for a normal single load in a washing machine. Lay the bundles in the hot water. Wearing the rubber boots, climb into the bath and stomp on the bundles for about five minutes to encourage a certain amount of felting. Drain the bath, then rinse the bundles several times with cold water to remove any trace of detergent.

- Spin the bundles dry if you have a washing machine, or squeeze them until you have removed as much water as possible if you do not. Open the bundles and lay the now

slightly felted wool on a drying rack for at least 12 hours to dry. Repeat until you have felted all four bags of roving.

- Once the wool is fully dry, pull the end of one length apart so that the roving is split evenly into two: as you gently pull, the roving should easily split down the entire length. Repeat this on each split length so that the original length is now split into four. Ball up your newly created yarn.

Pattern

Main piece

Cast on 25 sts.

Row 1: K5, [p5, k5] to end.

Row 2: P5, [k5, p5] to end.

Rep rows 1–2 twice more. *Row 6 completed*

Row 7: P5, [k5, p5] to end.

Row 8: K5, [p5, k5] to end.

Rep rows 7–8 twice more. *Row 12 completed*

Rep rows 1–12 twice more, then rep rows 1–6 once more.

Bind (cast) off.

To make up

- Using the bodkin, weave in all loose ends.
- Steam flat and shape into a rectangle.

→ **SPLITTING THE YARN**

When splitting the yarn, do this over a sheet as it will shed fibers.

Continental style: knit stitch

An alternative way of knitting is to hold the yarn in your left hand in the style known as Continental. This is how you make a knit stitch using this method.

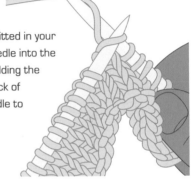

1 Hold the needle with the stitches to be knitted in your left hand. Insert the tip of the right-hand needle into the front of the first stitch from left to right. Holding the yarn fairly taut with your left hand at the back of your work, use the tip of the right-hand needle to pick up a loop of yarn.

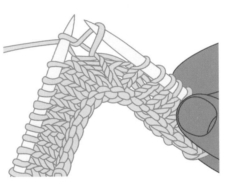

2 With the tip of the right-hand needle, bring the yarn through the original stitch to form a loop. This loop is your new stitch.

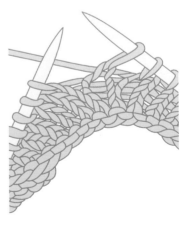

3 Slip the original stitch off the left-hand needle by gently pulling the right-hand needle to the right.

Repeat these three steps until all the stitches on the left-hand needle have been transferred to the right-hand needle. At the end of the row, swap the needles so that all the stitches are again in your left hand.

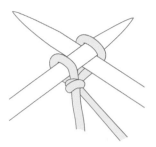

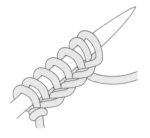

5 For every following stitch, insert the right-hand needle between the two previous stitches.

6 Repeat from * until you have the required number of stitches on the left-hand needle.

→ **EXTRA STITCHES**

To cast on extra stitches in the middle of a project, repeat the sequence from Step 5.

Knit stitch

This is the first and easiest stitch that a beginner will learn. Rows of knit stitches create garter stitch. The yarn should be held at the back of the work.

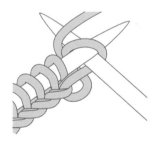

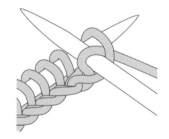

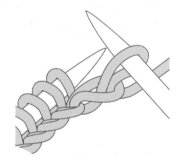

1 Hold the needle with the cast-on stitches in your left hand. Insert the right-hand needle into the front of the first stitch, from left to right (this is called "knitwise"), and take the yarn under and around the tip.

2 Use the tip of the right-hand needle to draw the loop through the stitch.

3 Slip the original stitch off the left-hand needle to complete the first knit stitch. Repeat these three steps until all the stitches on the left-hand needle have been transferred to the right-hand needle. At the end of the row, swap the needles so that all the stitches are again in your left hand.

Hot-air balloon

Instead of having all decoration kept to the walls, create this magical hanging for a bedroom ceiling. In soft sorbet shades, this pattern will work well for both boys and girls.

100

Skill level ★★

Size

15¾in (40cm) high (including basket) x 12in (30cm) diameter

Materials

Yarn

Fine 4ply yarn such as Pura Lana Baruffa 4ply from Robert Todd—100% extrafine merino wool; approx. 186yds (170m) per 1¾oz (50g) ball

- Canadian Goose (A)—2¼oz (60g)/240yds (200m)
- Aqua (B)—2¼oz (60g)/240yds (200m)
- Acid Green (C)—2¼oz (60g)/240yds (200m)

NOTE: Use two ends of yarn held together throughout

Soft DK yarn, such as Baby Alpaca from King Cole—100% baby alpaca: approx. 110 yds (100m) per 1¾oz (50g) ball

- Camel (D)—1oz (20g)/60yds (40m)

Needles

Set of four US 10½ (6.5mm) double-pointed knitting needles

32in (80cm) circular US 10½ (6.5 mm) needle

Pair of US 10½ (6.5mm) knitting needles

Other materials

- Polystyrene ball measuring 12 in (30cm), which comes in two halves
- Knitter's sewing needle
- Cord for attaching basket
- Fishing line for hanging
- Curtain ring for hanging
- PVA glue to stick halves of ball together
- 1¼in (3cm) square of scrap felt to glue inside ball to secure fishing line

Gauge (tension)

14 sts and 20 rows to 4in (10cm) over st st using US 10½ (6.5 mm) needles and two ends of yarn held together

Abbreviations

See page 126

Pattern

Balloon

Using US 10½ (6.5 mm) double-pointed needles and A, cast on 9 sts.

Evenly distribute sts over 3 double-pointed needles. Place a marker to denote end of round.

Round 1: Knit

Round 2: Inc in every st. *18 sts*

Round 3: [K1, inc] 9 times. *27 sts*

Round 4: [K2, inc] 9 times. *36 sts*

Round 5: [K3, inc] 9 times. *45 sts*

Round 6: [K4, inc] 9 times. *54 sts*

Round 7: [K5, inc] 9 times. *63 sts*

Round 8: [K6, inc] 9 times. *72 sts*

Round 9: [K7, inc] 9 times. *81 sts*

Round 10: [K8 inc] 9 times. *90 sts*

Round 11: [K9, inc] 9 times. *99 sts*

Round 12: [K10, inc] 9 times. *108 sts*

Round 13: [K11, inc] 9 times. *117 sts*

Rounds 14–18: Knit.

Round 19: [K12, inc] 9 times. *126 sts*

Transfer sts onto circular needle.

Change to B.

Rounds 20–23: Knit.

Change to A.

Rounds 24–26: Knit.

Change to C.

Rounds 27–35: Knit.

Change to B.

Rounds 36–38: Knit.

Change to C.

Rounds 39–45: Knit.

Change to A.

Rounds 46–49: Knit.

Change to B.

Rounds 50–56: Knit.

Change to C.

Rounds 57–59: Knit.

Change to A.

Rounds 60–64: Knit.

Change to knitting back and forth on straight needles

*****Row 65**: K12, k2tog, turn; work on these 13 sts and leave rem sts on circular needle.

Rows 66–70: Beg with a p row, work in st st.

Row 71: K11, k2tog. *12 sts*

Row 72: P2tog, p10. *11 sts*

Row 73: K9, k2tog. *10 sts*

Row 74: P2tog, p8. *9 sts*

Row 75: K7, k2tog. *8 sts*

Row 76: P2tog, p6. *7 sts*

Row 77: K5, k2tog. *6 sts*

Row 78: P2tog, p4. *5 sts*

Row 79: K3, k2tog. *4 sts*

Row 80: P2tog, p2. *3 sts*

Row 81: K1, k2tog. *2 sts*

Bind (cast) off for base of balloon.*

Rep from * to * 8 more times on separate groups of 13 sts at a time from circular needle.

Basket

Using US 10½ (6.5mm) needles and D, cast on 9 sts.

Row 1: K1, [p1, k1] to end.

This row is repeated to form seed (moss) st.

Work 35 more rows seed (moss) st.

Bind (cast) off.

First side

Pick up and knit 9 sts along right-hand edge between rows 14 and 23.

Work 13 rows seed (moss) st.

Bind (cast) off.

Second side

Work as for First Side, but on left-hand edge.

To make up

- Weave in all loose ends.
- On basket piece, using mattress stitch, sew up seams to form open-topped box.
- Steam balloon piece gently following instructions on yarn band.
- Sew 1yd (1m) length of fishing line to the felt square. From the flat side of one half-ball, thread the fishing line through the center to the outside, then glue the felt to the middle of the flat side with PVA. Leave to dry.
- Glue the halves of ball together.
- Cover the ball with knitted balloon piece and thread fishing line through center top. Attach curtain ring to end of line.
- Using matching yarn, sew segments together around base of balloon to completely cover the polystyrene.
- Attach basket with cords to base of knitted balloon.

NOTE: Ensure that you increase the height of the balloon above the crib before your baby is able to sit up or pull themselves up using the bars of the crib.

→ **KNITTING THE BALLOON**

Knitting the base of the balloon in segments allows you to slip the polystyrene ball inside it.

Snail cushion

This simple coil cushion, made into a fun snail, is a perfect first knitting project. You can use it as a cushion, or even as a knitted toy.

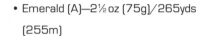

Skill level ★

Size

12 in (30cm) diameter

Materials

Yarn

Fine 4ply yarn such as Pura Lana Baruffa 4ply from Robert Todd—100% extrafine merino wool; approx. 186yds (170m) per 1¾oz (50g) ball

- Emerald (A)—2½oz (75g)/265yds (255m)
- Aqua (B)—2½oz (75g)/265yds (255m)
- Canadian Goose (C)—1¾oz (50g)/186yds (170m)

NOTE: Use two ends of yarn held together throughout

Needles

Pair of US 7 (4.5 mm) knitting needles

Other materials

- Toy stuffing
- Knitter's sewing needle

Gauge (tension)

19 sts and 25 rows to 4in (10cm) over st st using US 7 (4.5 mm) needles and two ends of yarn held together

Abbreviations

See page 126

Pattern

Main piece

Using A, cast on 20 sts.

*__Rows 1–20:__ Knit.

Change to B.

Rows 21–40: Knit.*

Rep from * to * 12 more times, or until the work measures approx. 43in (110cm).

Change to C.

Beg with a k row, work 52 rows st st.

Next row: [K3, inc] 5 times. *25 sts*

Next row: Purl.

Next row: [K4, inc] 5 times. *30 sts*

Next row: Purl.

Next row: [K5, inc] 5 times. *35 sts*

Beg with a p row, work 9 rows st st.

Next row: [K5, k2tog] 5 times. *30 sts*

Next row: Purl.

Next row: [K4, k2tog] 5 times. *25 sts*

Next row: Purl.

Next row: [K3, k2tog] 5 times. *20 sts*

Next row: Purl.

Next row: [K2, k2tog] 5 times. *15 sts*

Next row: Purl.

Next row: [K1, k2tog] 5 times *10 sts*

Thread end through rem 10 sts, pull tight, and secure end.

To make up

• Weave in all loose ends.

• Steam gently following instructions on yarn band.

• Sew edges together to create long tube, stuffing it evenly in sections as you go.

• With seam facing inward stitch into coil shape, using photograph as a guide.

→ GIANT SNAIL

It would be very easy to make this into a larger floor cushion... just keep knitting.

Chunky knit bolster

This super-simple pattern is given a quirky and modern twist by using a yarn made from the off-cuts of jersey fabric. It comes in solid or stripe colorways, each giving a unique result.

106

Skill level ★

Size
20in x 6in (51cm x 15cm)

Materials
Yarn
Stretchy jersey fabric yarn such as Hooplayarn from Hoopla—100% cotton jersey; approx. 110yds (100m) per 17½oz (500g) ball
- Zebra—approx. 17½oz (500g)/110yds (100m)

OR
- Deep Blue—approx. 17½oz (500g)/110yds (100m)

Needles
Pair of US 15 (10mm) knitting needles

Other materials
- Bolster pad measuring 18in (45cm) long by 6¾in (17cm) diameter
- Knitter's sewing needle

Gauge (tension)
7 sts and 14 rows to 4in (10cm) over garter stitch using US 15 (10mm) needles

Abbreviations
See page 126

Pattern
Main piece
Cast on 47 sts.
Row 1: K45, turn.
Row 2: K43, turn.

→ GAUGE (TENSION)

Because this "yarn" is made from off-cuts from the textile industry, the stretch varies depending on the color. Don't worry too much about the gauge (tension)—just knit to your natural gauge (tension).

Row 3: K41, turn.

Row 4: K39, turn.

Row 5: K37, turn.

Row 6: K35, turn.

Row 7: Knit to end.

Row 8: Knit to end.

Rep rows 1–8, 7 more times.
Bind (cast) off.

To make up

• Weave in loose ends.

• Insert bolster pad into cavity of the
  knit and join cast-on and bound-

(cast-) off edges with knitting yarn to
form cylindrical shape. Gather ends
and secure.

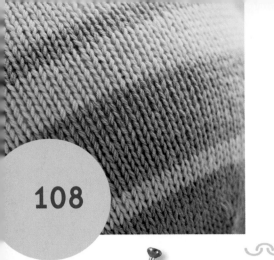

Equipment and Techniques

On the following pages you'll find instructions for all the knitting and crochet skills you'll need in order to make any of the projects.

Basic knitting equipment

The projects in this book require only the simplest tools to make them.

Single-point knitting needles come in various sizes and materials. The size required is given in each pattern, but the material is a personal choice for the knitter. Beginners often find bamboo needles easiest because they are less slippery than metal or plastic knitting needles.

Double-pointed knitting needles (DPNs) are used in sets of four or five (sets of four are fine for the projects in this book) and allow you to knit off both ends in order to knit in the round (see page 117).

A **cable needle** is used to hold a group of stitches at the front or back of the work while working a cable twist (see page 116). The size should correspond with the size of knitting needles being used. You can get cranked cable needles, like this one, which are easier to use than straight cable needles if you are a beginner knitter.

A **knitter's sewing needle** (or a **tapestry needle** if the yarn is fine) is used to sew together pieces of knitting (see page 118). These needles have blunt ends to help prevent them splitting the yarn.

Knitting techniques

The following pages show you all the techniques you need to get you started on the projects in this book.

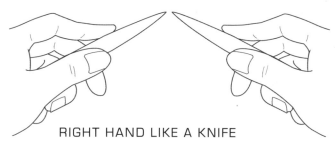

Holding needles and yarn

Every knitter will develop their own style, but there are two popular ways to hold the knitting needles. Try them both and adopt the style that feels more natural for you.

RIGHT HAND LIKE A KNIFE

Pick up the needles in both hands as you would a knife and fork, with the needles running under the palms of your hands. You will need to let go of the knitting with your right hand—tuck the blunt end of the needle under your arm to hold it—in order to move the yarn around the tip of the needle.

RIGHT HAND LIKE A PEN

Keeping the left hand in the same position, hold the right-hand needle as you would hold a pen, with the needle resting in the crook of your hand. This position has the advantage that you can control the yarn with your right index finger without letting go of the needles.

HOLDING THE YARN

In order to create even knitting the yarn will need to be tensioned. You can wrap the yarn differently around your fingers depending on your natural gauge (tension), but try this method first because it works for most people. Wind the yarn around your little finger and lace it over the ring finger, under the second finger and over the first finger. The right-hand index finger will be used to wind the yarn around the needle point.

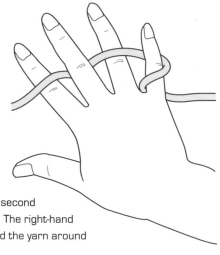

Slip knot

Every piece of knitting starts with a simple slip knot.

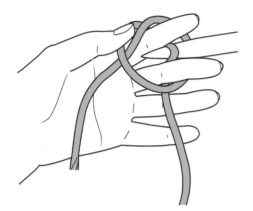

1 Leaving about a 4in (10cm) tail of yarn, wind yarn twice around two fingers of your left hand. Slip the tip of a knitting needle between your fore and second fingers and under the loop furthest from the fingertips, as shown. Draw this loop through the other loop.

2 Pull on the ends of the yarn to tighten the loop on the needle; this has created the first stitch.

Casting on (cable method)

I usually use the cable method to cast on stitches: this technique can be used in all projects in this book and creates a neat, firm edge.

1 Hold needle with slip knot in your left hand. Insert the tip of the right-hand needle from left to right into the front of the knot.

2 *Wrap the yarn under and around the tip of the right-hand needle.

3 Draw the yarn through to form a new stitch on the right-hand needle.

4 Slip this stitch from the right-hand needle onto the left-hand needle.